**AFRICA**

MW00424720

What Comes To Mind
When You Think of Africa?

Take a surprising look at urban cities on the continent of Africa.

NAPOLEAN GIVENS
(Sr.)

Countries' worldwide have said that Africa needs saving, but contrary to these world views, Akon has pointed out in a public interview that it's Africa that's doing the saving.

"Every natural resource that's been keeping every country in the world operating has some resource that's been pulled from Africa".

AKON

Music Mogul, singer and activist

"African Cities is a book I consider to be well on point, interesting and very much intriguing"

James L. Foxx

Former Academic Scholar/Writer

"A great book and is very informative. It's not about jungles and primitive people. A book that's other than a safari" in Africa.

Ronald L. Bridges

Black Culture/Historian

"African Cities...What Comes to Mind When You Think of Africa by Napolean Givens; I find to be a good book for reference"

Herschel Willis

Writer; Commentator

WHAT COME TO MIND
WHEN YOU THINK OF AFRICA?

Much more than a safari vacation, over 21 developed cities are described along
with interesting facts and figures about the world's richest continent.

NAPOLEAN GIVENS

Foreword..................i

Acknowledgement............ii

Introduction.................. iii

Kings & Queens of Africa.........83

AFRICAN CITIES

NAPOLEAN GIVENS
(Sr.)

Foreword

There is nowhere on planet earth a place quite like Africa. From its vast savannahs to its teeming cities, it is a continent of extreme on the one hand and unparalleled beauty on the other. Where will Africa be in the next 40 years? Will our Children be engaging with this rich continent of boundless opportunities and resources? Or will they grow up with their backs turned to it?

In today's time, our kids will be facing a more diverse and connected world than ever before when they graduate. They will not only be competing with kids in their own country or cities but the world for jobs. This is why cultural literacy has become increasingly important for our kids to learn more about the abundant in modern-day African cities. Africa offers a new promise and opportunities the likes the world has never seen before and shouldn't turn a blind eye on them.

Today, China has turned its interest heavily on developing a business relationship with Africa attempting to get ahead of our country. But the continent of Africa is more open to working with the USA. We should not allow our children to lag behind this new paradigm shift in global economic opportunities due to our nation's misconceptions about Africa. We will begin by taking a modern-day look at urban cities inside of Africa to help clear up many of its miss-representation while gaining some new perspective. Let's us now turn to the new possibilities this vast continent present when we think of Africa.

Acknowledgement

They say nothing great happens without the help of others along the way and so it is with this book compilation. I owe thanks and gratitude to a host of close friends, strangers, cousins, business associate and too many of my spiritual brothers and sisters in the ministries. I dedicate this book to their work challenges. I thank the Almighty above I'd had the privilege to present this book on African Cities. And I thank Him for placing me among marvelous people that served as guiding lights in the path of my life journey.

Last, but not least and most important in my life is my family, who has done so much to tolerate me in my pursuit, yet love me enough to stick with me while I explore my innermost passion to create.

Introduction

The purpose of this book is to present African cities as a global economy from within its urban cities on the continent of Africa. Rather than as a traveler, booking airline tickets reservation to one of Africa Great Safari or vacation tour of its ancient wonders, it's our hope, that African cities will become a rich and favorable alternative that comes to mind when you think of Africa.

If you have ever lived in America for any length of time, you have seen these horrific images of Africa, its land and its people. Broadcast over America mainstream media, these images are often portrayed as though the whole continent of Africa is all wild and primitive. Many people have grown up accustomed to this.

Just a glimpse through the pages of this book, you will find Africa to be quite contrary to how it's been widely portrayed. I hope this book broadens your perspective and enlighten your thoughts about Africa. And though this book is not a tell-all book, is designed to help you along your way in discovering more about urban cities inside the continent of Africa. I believe you will find Africa to be an amazing continent, full of promise the world has yet to see in African cities modernization.

While it's not the broader scope of this book, Africa is home to some of the world oldest ancient kingdoms and civilizations. I decided to devote the final chapter of this book to some of the Great Kings and Queens of Africa that once reigned over its land. This can be your introduction to Africa's glorious ancient past.

May I add, within the last 2 years, I conducted an independent survey of adults of all ages, including children from kindergarten to k 12, and asked the question that's in the title of this book?

What comes to mind when you think of Africa? Top three answers:

Tacky huts   *Extreme poverty*   *and*   *Wild jungles*

What so alarming about the above answers in this survey, is that the same question was ask of these kids from kindergarten to k-12, and their answers more or less reflect the same answers as the adult group.

However, I must admit in subsequent surveys, the answers to the question above depended largely on whom I ask and what ethnic core group I presented it to. To many folks, Africa is home sweet home and to its many visitors', it's a great place to go experience Africa's ancient wonders and open wildlife in their national parks up close. My initial survey focuses primarily on minorities and Hispanic as core groups and their views were quite remarkable and contrary to other ethnic groups.

With that said, you will discover that Africa is much more than tacky huts, wild jungles, and extreme poverty. The rich continent of Africa has urban developed cities very much like our own and any tourist visiting there will tell you this. It's a land of untold riches and ancient history; we all can gain a greater appreciation for it.

Finally, it's worth noting, this book did not happen overnight. It took 3 long painstaking years to research and developed. A lot of the content was changing and expanding as I was gathering it. This book represents the best and most current information I could muster up before publication. This is the first edition, so it is far from perfection but future edition will reflect improve changes and updates.

Kings & Queens of Africa

In the final chapters of this book, I explore some of the great Kings and Queens of Africa. In my updated edition, I will be exploring in more depth about the ancient Kings and Queens in my book "**Africa**" *From Ancient Time to Modern Day Cities*. The final chapters in this book are designed as an introduction to Africa's glorious past.

DAKAR, SENEGAL

Dakar is the capital city of Senegal, located on the Cape Verde Peninsula, on the country's Atlantic coast. It is Senegal's largest city. Its position on the western edge of Africa (it is the western most African city) and is an advantageous departure point for trans-Atlantic and European trade, this fact aided its growth into a major regional port.

According to official most recent estimates, the city of Dakar has a population of 1,303,594, whereas the population of the Dakar metropolitan area is estimated at 2.45 million people.

Dakar is a major administrative centre, home to the Nat'l Assembly of Senegal and the Senegal Presidential Palace. Dakar was under French colonial governance during the early 1900's.

What is Dakar known for?

Bustling, colorful **Senegal** is one of West Africa's most popular destinations, and also one of the regions safest. The capital **Dakar**, is a vibrant city famous for its lively markets and rich musical culture.

The Cap-Vert peninsula was settled no later than the 15th century, by the Lebou people, an aqua-cultural ethnic group related to the neighboring Wolof and Serer. The original villages: Ouakam, Ngor, Yoff and Hann, all still constitute distinctively Lebou neighborhoods of the city today. In 1444, the Portuguese reached the Bay of Dakar, initially as slave-raiders. Peaceful contact was finally opened in 1456 by Diogo Gomes, and the bay was subsequently referred to as the "Angrade Bezeguiche" (after the name of the local ruler).

The bay of "Bezeguiche" would go on to serve as a critical step for the Portuguese India Armadas of the early 16th century, where large fleets would routinely stop, both on their outward and return journeys from India, to repair, collect fresh water from the rivulets and wells along the Cap-Vert shore and trade for provisions with the local people for their remaining voyage (It was famously during one of these stops, in 1501, where the Florentine navigator Amerigo Vespucci began to construct his "New World" hypothesis about America.

The Portuguese eventually founded a settlement on the island of Gorée (then known as the island of Bezeguiche or Palma), which by 1536 they began to use as a base for slave exportation.

Bonus! Would you like to see the African Cities pics described inside this book in color? *FREE!* Color pic download. Go to: Africancitytravel@gmail.com (request African cities color pics)

KAMPALA, UGANDA

Kampala is the capital city of Uganda. With a population of 1,680,800 makes it the largest city in Uganda, as of its 2019 consensus. It is coterminous with the district of Kampala. The city is divided into five boroughs that oversee local planning: Central, Kawempe, Makindye, Nakawa and Rubaga.

The city grew as the capital of the Buganda kingdom, from which several buildings survive, including the Kasubi Tombs (built in the year of 1881, the Buganda parliament, the Buganda "Court of Justice and Naggalabi Buddo Coronation Site.

Severely damaged in the Uganda-Tanzania War, the city has since been rebuilt, with constructions of new buildings including hotels, shopping malls, educational institutions, banks, hospitals and improvement of war-torn buildings and infrastructure.

The main campus of Makerere University, one of East and Central Africa's premier institutes of higher learning can be found in the Makerere Hill area of the city. Kampala is also home to the headquarters of the African Development.

Kampala is reported to be among the fastest-growing cities in Africa, with an annual population growth rate of 4.03 percent by City Mayors. Kampala has been ranked the best city to live in East Africa ahead of Nairobi and Kigali by Mercer, a global development consulting agency based in New York City.

Historical Background

Kampala originally referred to only the present-day Old Kampala hill on whose summit was located the former Fort Lugard and the headquarters of the British Colonialist in the soon to be Uganda Protectorate. Before the British occupation and construction of Fort Lugard, this hill was a hunting reserve of the Kabaka of Buganda and had several species of antelope, especially the impala. When the British arrived, they called this place "The Hill of the Impala". Later on, the Baganda in whose territory this British Settlement was located, translated "Hill of the Impala" as Akasozike 'Empala – "Kasozi" meaning "hill", "ke" meaning "of", and "empala" the plural of "impala". In Luganda, the language of the Baganda, the words "kampala" meant "place of the impala" and hence the word "Kampala" came to refer to the British colonial Settlement that later developed out of the occupied Old Kampala hill near the pre-existing Kibuga (capital) of Buganda Kingdom.

This area of numerous hills that later become known as Kampala was the core of the highly centralized Buganda Kingdom and site of the of shifting Kibuga (capital) the different Basse kabaka (Kings) of Buganda Kingdom with each Kabaka (king) upon their coronation or subsequently during their reign setting up their Kibuga (capital) on a new and or different hill as their wished or desired.

The first written description of this Kibuga (capital) was by the explorer Richard Francis Burton in his book The Lake Region of East Africa published in 1860. In the book, Burton relying on the information collected by Snay Bin Amir, an Arab trader, described the Kibuga as

...the settlement is not less than a day's journey in length, the buildings are of cane and rattan. The sultan (Kabaka) palace is at least a mile long and the circular huts neatly arranged in a line are surrounded by a strong fence that has only four gates.

In 1862, when explorer John Speke arrived in the Buganda Kingdom, Mutesa I of the Buganda was king and his Kibuga (Capital) was at Banda barogo present-day Banda Hill.

In 1875 explorer Henry Morton Stanley reported the capital as being at present-day Lubaga hill where he met the same Kabaka Mutesa I. During this visit, Henry Morton Stanley wrote a letter that was published in the Daily Telegraphy inviting missionaries to come to Buganda and also described the Kibuga in his 1870's dispatches to the New York Herald, thus...

In 1897, Kampala's first Western-style health facility Mengo Hospital was opened on Namirembe hill by British Doctor and missionary Sir Albert Ruskin Cook later on founded Mulago Hospital the current National Referral Hospital in 1913 at Mulago hill. In 1899, Missionary Sisters of Our Lady of Africa founded Lubaga Hospital at Lubaga hill.

This agreement by Sir Harry Johnston created new land tenures such as Freehold, Crownland, Mailo and divided up and allocated the land in such a way would that would come to define the development of Kampala.

In 1922, Makerere University Kampala's oldest University was founded as the Uganda Technical College at the present Makerere hill and offered carpentry, building construction and mechanics, arts, education, agriculture, and medicine.

In 1930, another planning scheme (land use plan) was introduced to regulate developments within the township. The 1930 land-use plan for Kampala segregated residential, industrial and commercial areas as well as a planned civic center. The first sewerage plan was prepared to target a population of 20,000 people in Nakasero and Old Kampala areas of the Kampala Township. This plan guided sewerage development from 1936–1940 in planned urban areas of the Kampala Township and excluded the Kibuga area occupied by the Baganda and other natives.

In 1931, The Uganda Railway line reached Kampala connecting Kampala to Mombasa Port thirty-five years from the commencement of its construction.

In 1938, The East African Power & Lighting Company was granted a license for thermal electric power generation and distribution for towns of Kampala and Entebbe and in the same year Governor Sir Philip Mitchel switched on Kampala and Uganda's first electric street lights.

AFRICAN CITIES
FACT CHECK #1

Africa is known around the world as the Mother of
Civilization.

Leading scientist have found the oldest human fossils
dating back to over 100,000 years on the continents of
Africa.

Some have concluded they have found fossils dating back
"Several Million Years".

ADDIS ABABA

Addis Ababa, is the capital and largest city of Ethiopia according to the 2007 census, the city has a population of 2,739,551 inhabitants. As a chartered city, Addis Ababa also serves as a capital city of Oromia. It is where the African Union is headquartered and where its predecessor the Organization of African Unity (OAU) was based. It also hosts the headquarters of the "United Nations Economic Commission for Africa" as well as various other continental and international organizations. Addis Ababa is therefore often referred to as "the political capital of Africa" for its historical, diplomatic and political significance for the continent. The city lies a few miles west of the East African Rift which splits Ethiopia into two, through the Nubian Plate and the Somali Plate. The city is populated by people from different regions of Ethiopia. It is home to Addis Ababa University.

Mount Entoto is one of a handful of sites put forward as a possible location for a medieval imperial capital known as Barara. This permanent fortified city was established during the early-to-mid 15th century, and it served as the main residence of several successive emperors up to the early 16th-century reign of Lebna Dengel.

The city was depicted standing between Mounts Zikwala and Menegasha on a map drawn by the Italian cartographer Fra Mauro in around 1450, and it was razed and plundered by

Ahmed Gragn while the imperial army was trapped on the south of the Awash River in 1529, an event witnessed and documented two years later by the Yemeni writer Arab-Faqih.

The suggestion that Barara was located on Mount Entoto is supported by the very recent discovery of a large medieval town overlooking Addis Ababa located between rock-hewn Washa Mikael and the more modern church of Entoto Maryam, founded in the late 19th century by Emperor Menelik. Dubbed the Pentagon, the 30-hectare site incorporates a castle with 12 towers, along with 520 meters of stone walls measuring up to 5 meter high. The site of Addis Ababa was chosen by Empress Taytu Betul and the city was founded in 1886 by Emperor Menelik II, as initially a King of the Shewa province, had found Mount Entoto a useful base for military operations in the south of his realm, and in 1879 he visited the reputed ruins of a medieval town and an unfinished rock church that showed proof of the medieval empire's capital.

FREETOWN CAPE SIERRA

Freetown, is locally governed by the <u>Freetown City Council</u>, headed by a mayor. The mayor and members of the Freetown City Council are directly elected by the residents of Freetown in elections held every four years. The current mayor of Freetown is Yvonne Aki Sawyers, who was sworn in on May 11, 2018, after her victory in the 2018 Freetown Mayoral election. The Freetown city council has its own <u>municipal police</u> force.

The city of Freetown is divided into three municipal regions; the East End, Central, and the West End, which in turns are divided into 8 <u>electoral wards</u>: East I, East II, East III, and Central I, Central II, West I, West II, and West III. The East End is both the most populous, and the most densely populous of the three regions within Freetown.

Historical background

In 1791, Thomas Peters, an African American who had served in the <u>Black Pioneers</u>, went to England to report the grievances of the black population in <u>Nova Scotia</u>. Some of these African Americans were ex-slaves who had escaped to the British forces who had been given their freedom and resettled there by the Crown after the <u>American Revolution</u>. Land grants and assistance in starting the settlements had been intermittent and slow. During his visit, Peters met with the directors of the <u>Sierra Leone Company</u> and learned of proposals for a new settlement at Sierra Leone. Despite the collapse of the 1787 colony, the directors were eager to recruit settlers to Sierra Leone. <u>Lieutenant John Clarkson, RN</u>, who was an abolitionist, was sent to Nova Scotia in British North America to register immigrants to take to Sierra Leone for a new settlement.

Tired of the harsh weather and racial discrimination in Nova Scotia, more than 1,100 former American slaves chose to go to Sierra Leone. They sailed in 15 ships and arrived in St. George Bay between February 26 and March 9th, 1792. Sixty-four settlers died en-route to Sierra Leone, and Lieutenant Clarkson was among those taken ill during the voyage. Upon reaching Sierra Leone, Clarkson along with some of the Nova Scotian 'captains' "dispatched onshore to clear or make roadway for their landing". The Nova Scotians were to build Freetown on the former site of the first Granville Town, where the jungle had taken over since its destruction in 1789. Its surviving Old Settlers had relocated to Fourah Bay in 1791.

At Freetown, the women remained in the ships while the men worked to clear the land. Lt. Clarkson told the men to clear the land until they reached a large cotton tree. After the work had been done and the land cleared, all the Nova Scotians, men and women disembarked and marched towards the thick forest and to the cotton tree, and their preachers (all African Americans) began singing "Awake and Sing of Moses and the Lamb."

AFRICAN CITIES
FACT CHECK #2

Obama Achieving the Dream

The 44th president of the United States
(And the first elected black president in U.S. history)

President Obama father was a native of Africa, a graduate of Harvard College who died in a tragic car accident while in Africa before his son Obama successful run for president.

The former president has a surviving stepbrother, grandmother and host of relatives and friends on the continent of Africa.

"Africa changes you forever, like nowhere on earth. Once you have been there, you will never be the same. But how do you begin to describe its magic to someone who has never felt it: How can you explain the fascination of this vast, dusty continent, whose oldest roads are elephant paths: Could it be because Africa is the place of all our beginnings, the cradle of mankind, where our species first stood upright on the savannahs of long ago?"

Brian Jackman

Writer, Journalist,

CAIRO, EGYPT

Cairo, is the capital of Egypt. The city's metropolitan area is one of the largest in Africa, the largest in the Middle East and 15th-largest in the world, and is associated with ancient Egypt, as the famous Giza pyramid complex and the ancient city of Memphis are located in its geographical area. Located near the Nile Delta, modern Cairo was founded in 969 AD by the Fatimid dynasty, but the land composing the present-day city was the site of ancient national capitals whose remnants remain visible in parts of Old Cairo. Cairo has long been a Centre of the region's political and cultural life and is titled "the city of a thousand minarets" for its preponderance of Islamic architecture. Cairo is considered a World City with a "Beta +" classification according to GaWC.

Cairo has the oldest and largest film and music industries in the Middle East, as well as the world's second-oldest institution of higher learning, Al-Azhar University. The Arab League has had its headquarters in Cairo for most of its existence. And many international media, businesses, and organizations have regional headquarters in the city;

With a population of over 9 million spread over 3,085 square kilometers (1,191 sq. mi), Cairo is by far the largest city in Egypt. An additional 9.5 million inhabitants live in close proximity to the city. Cairo, like many other megacities, suffers from high levels of pollution and traffic. Cairo's metro, one of two in Africa (the other being in Algiers, Algeria), ranks among the fifteen busiest in the world, with over 1 billion annual passenger rides. The economy of Cairo was ranked first in the Middle East in 2005, and 43rd globally on *Foreign Policy*'s 2010 Global Cities Index.

Egyptians quite often refer to Cairo as *Maṣr*, the Egyptian Arabic name for Egypt itself, emphasizing the city's importance for the country. Its official name *al-Qāhirah*☐ (Arabicةر) means "the Vanquisher" or "the Conqueror", supposedly due to the fact that the planet Mars, *an-Najm al-Qāhir* (Arabic: "the Conquering Star"), was rising at the time when the city was being founded, possibly also in reference to the much awaited arrival of the Fatimid Caliph Al-Mu'izz who reached Cairo from Mahdia in 973, the old Fatimid capital. The location of the ancient city of <u>Heliopolis</u> is the suburb of Ain Shams (Arabic: عين شمس, "Eye of the Sun"). The Coptic name of the city is Kashromiwhich means "main breaker".

Cairo is located on the banks and islands of the Nile River in the north of Egypt, just south of the point where the river leaves its desert-bound valley and breaks into two branches into the low lying Nile Delta region. West of Giza, in the desert is part of the ancient recropolis of Memphis on the Giza plateau, with its three large pyramids, including the Great Pyramid of Giza.

ASMARA, Eritrea

Asmara or **Asmera,** is the capital and most populous city of Eritrea, in the country's Central Region. The city is located at the tip of the escarpment that is both the northwestern edge of the Eritrean Highlands and the Great Rift Valley inside of neighbouring Ethiopia. It sits at an elevation of 2,325 meters (7,628 ft.), thus making it the sixth highest capital in the world by altitude. In 2017, the city was officially declared as a _UNESCO WORLD HERITAGE_ site for its well-preserved modernist architecture.

Historical background

Asmera was first settled in 800 BC with a population ranging from 100 to 1000. The city was then founded in the 12th century AD after four separate villages united to live together peacefully after originally, according to Eritrean Tigrinya oral traditional history, four clans were living in the Asmera area on the Kebessa Plateau: the Gheza Gurtom, the Gheza Shelele, the Gheza Serenser, and Gheza Asmae.

These towns were frequently attacked by clans from the low land and from the rulers of "seger mereb melash" (which now is a Tigray region in Ethiopia) until the women of each clan decided that to defeat their common enemy and preserve peace the four clans must unite. The men accepted, hence the name "Arbate Asmera". Arbate Asmera literally means, in the Tigrinya language, "the four (feminine plural) made them unite". Eventually, Arbate was dropped and it has now been called Asmera which means "they feminine, thus referring to the women made them unite". There is still a district called Arbaete Asmera in the Administrations of Asmara. It is now called the Italianized version of the word Asmara. The westernized version of the name is used by a majority of non-Eritreans, while the multilingual inhabitants of Eritrea and neighbouring peoples remain loyal to the original pronunciation, Asmera.

Asmera, a small village in the nineteenth century, started to grow quickly when it was occupied by Italy in1889. Governor Ferdinando Martini made it the capital city of Italian Eritrea in 1900.

In the early 20th century, the Eritrean Railway was built to the coast, passing through the town of Ghinda, under the direction of Carlo Cavanna. In both 1913 and 1915, the city suffered only slight damage in large earthquakes
.

A large Italian community developed the city. According to the 1939 census, Asmera had a population of 98,000, of which 53,000 were Italian. Only 75,000 Italians lived in all of Eritrea, making the capital city by far their largest Centre. (Compare this to the Italian colonization of Libya, where the settler population, albeit larger, was more dispersed).

The capital acquired an Italian architectural look. Europeans used Asmera "to experiment with radical new designs". By late 1930s, Asmera was called *Piccola Roma.*

DAR-ES SALAAM TANZANIA

Dar es Salaam *Dār as-Salām*, ('house of peace'), or simply **Dar**, formerly known as **Mzizim** is also the former capital as well as the most populous city in Tanzania and a regionally important economic Centre. Located on the Swahili coast, the city is one of the fastest-growing' cities in the world.

Until 1974, Dar es Salaam served as Tanzania's capital city, at which point the capital city commenced transferring to Dodoma, which was officially completed in 1996. However, as of 2018, it remains a focus of central government bureaucracy, although this is in the process of fully moving to Dodoma. It is Tanzania's most prominent city in arts, fashion, media, music, film, and television, and is a leading financial Centre. The city is the leading arrival and departure point for most tourists who visit Tanzania, including the national parks for safaris and the islands of Unguja and Pemba.

In the 19th century, **Mzizima** (Swahili for "healthy town") was a coastal fishing village on the periphery of Indian Ocean trade routes. In 1865, 1866, Sultan Majid bin Said of Zanzibar began building a new city very close to Mzizima and named it **Dar es Salaam**. The name is commonly translated as "abode/ home of peace", based on the Arabic *dar* ("house"), and the Arabic *el salaam* ("of peace"). Dar es Salaam also fell into their decline after Majid's death in 1870, but was revived in 1887 when the German East

25

Africa Company established a station there. The town's growth was facilitated by its role as the administrative and commercial Centre of German East Africa and industrial expansion resulting from the construction of the Central Railway Line in the early 1900s.

German East Africa was captured by the British during World War I and became Tanganyika with Dar el Salaam remaining the administrative and commercial Centre. Under British indirect rule, separate European (Oyster Bay) and African (e.g., Kariakoo and Ilala) areas developed at a distance from the city Centre. After World War II, Dar es Salaam experienced a period of rapid growth.

The Tanzania Ports Authority (TPA, under construction) and PSPF Pension Twin Towers, both in the background, are the tallest in East and Central Africa. It is the capital of the co-extensive Dar es Salaam Region, which is one of Tanzania's 31 administrative regions and consists overall of five districts: Kinondoni located in the north Ilala in the Centre, Ubungo and Temeke in the south and Kigamboni in the east across the Kurasini creek. The region had a population of 4,364,541 as of the official 2012 census.

NAIROBI, KENYA

Nairobi (/naɪˈroʊbi/) is the capital and the largest city of Kenya. The two other major cities inside Kenya are the port city of Mombasa along the Indian Ocean coast and the lake port city of Kisumu inside the Western Kenya on Lake Victoria's Winam Gulf. The name Nairobi comes from the Maasai phrase *Enkare Nairobi*, which translates to "cool water", a reference to the Nairobi River which flows through the city. The city had a population of 3,138,369 in the 2009 census, while the metropolitan area has a population of 6,547,547. The city is popularly referred to as the Green City in the Sun.

Historical background

Nairobi was founded in 1899 by the colonial authorities in British East Africa, as a rail depot on the Uganda Railway. The town quickly grew to replace Mombasa as the capital of Kenya in 1907. After independence in 1963, Nairobi became the capital of the Republic of Kenya. During Kenya's colonial period, the city became a Centre for the colony's coffee, tea, and sisal industry. The city lies on the River Athi in the southern part of the country and has an elevation of 1,795 meters (5,889 ft.) above sea level.

On 9/11 1973, the Kenyatta International Conference Centre KICC was open to the public. The 28-story building at the time was designed by the Norwegian architect Karl Henrik Nøstvik and Kenyan David Mutiso. The construction was done in three phases. Phase I was the construction of the podium, Phase II consisted of the main tower, and Phase III involved the Plenary. Construction was completed in 1973, with the ceremonial opening occurring on 9/11 and being presided over by Kenya's founding father President Kenyatta. It is the only building within the city with a helipad that is open to the public.

Of the buildings built in the Seventies, the KICC was the most eco-friendly and most environmentally conscious structure; its mainframe was constructed with locally available materials gravel, sand, cement, and wood, and it had wide-open spaces which allowed for natural aeration and natural lighting. Cuboids made up the plenary hall, the tower consisted of a cylinder composed of several cuboids, and the Amphitheatre and helipad both resembled cones. The tower was built around a concrete core and it had no walls but glass windows, which allowed for maximum natural lighting. It had the largest halls in eastern and central Africa.

Three years prior in 1972, the World Bank approved funds for further expansion of the then Nairobi Airport now (Jomo Kenyatta International Airport), including a new international and domestic passenger terminal building, the airport's first dedicated cargo and freight terminal, new taxiways, associated aprons, internal roads, car parks, police and fire stations, a State Pavilion, airfield and roadway lighting, residential fire hydrant system, water, electrical, telecommunications and sewage systems, a dual carriageway passenger access road, security, drainage and the building of the main access road to the airport (Airport South Road). The total cost of the project was more than US$29 million (US$111.8 million in 2013 dollars). On 14 March 1978, construction of the current terminal building was completed on the other side of the airport's single runway and opened by President Jomo Kenyatta less than five months before his death. The airport was renamed Jomo Kenyatta International Airport in memory of its First President.

The United States Embassy, then located in downtown Nairobi, was bombed in August 1998 by Al-Qaida, as one of a series of US embassy bombings. It's now the site of a memorial park.

With a population growth of 3.36 million in 2011, Nairobi is the second-largest city by population in the *African Great Lakes* region after Dar es Salaam, Tanzania. According to the 2009 census bureau, in the administrative area of Nairobi, 3,138,295 inhabitants presently lived within 696 km 269 sq. mi. Nairobi is the 10th-largest city in Africa, including the population of its suburbs.

Home to thousands of Kenyan businesses and over 100 major international companies and organizations, including the United Nations Environment programed (UN Environment) and the United Nations Office at Nairobi (UNON), Nairobi is an established hub for business and culture. The (NSE) Nairobi Securities Exchange is one of the largest in Africa and the second-oldest exchange on the continent. It is Africa's fourth-largest exchange in terms of trading volume, capable of making 10 million trades a day.

AFRICAN CITIES
FACT CHECK #3

		Population (approximate)
United States........3.6 million sq. miles		327 M
China...................3.7 million sq miles.......1.417 B		
Russia..................6.6 million sq. miles..........145 M		
Africa..................12 million sq. miles........1.216 B		

M - Million
B - Billion

MAJOR CONTINENT COUNTRY COMPARED   Source / Odyssey III Atlass

MONROVIA, LIBERIA

Monrovia /mən'roʊviə/ the capital city of the West African country of Liberia. Located on the Atlantic Coast at Cape Mesurado, Monrovia had a population of 1,010,970 as of the 2008 census. With 29% of the total population of Liberia, Monrovia is the country's most populous city.

Founded on April 25, 1822, Monrovia was the second permanent Black African American settlement in Africa after Freetown, Sierra Leone. Monrovia's economy is shaped primarily by its harbour and its role as the location of Liberia's government offices.

Monrovia is named in honour of President James Monroe, of the United States, a prominent supporter of the colonization of Liberia and the American Colonization Society. Along with Washington, D.C., it is one of two national capitals to be named after a U.S. President.

Monrovia lies along the Cape Mesurado peninsula, between the Atlantic Ocean and the Mesurado River, whose mouth forms a large natural harbor. The Saint Paul River lies directly north of the city and forms the northern boundary of Bushrod Island, which is reached by crossing the "New Bridge" from downtown Monrovia. Monrovia is located in Montserrado County and is Liberia's largest city and its administrative, commercial and financial centre.

The city of Monrovia consists of several districts, spread across the Mesurado peninsula, with the greater Metropolitan area encircling the marshy Mesurado River's mouth. The historic downtown, centred on Broad Street, is at the very end of the peninsula, with the major market district, Waterside, immediately to the north, facing the city's large natural harbour.

Northwest of Waterside is the large, low-income West Point community. To the west/southwest of downtown lies Mamba Point, traditionally the city's principal diplomatic quarter, and home to the Embassies of the United States and the United Kingdom as well as the Delegation of European Union. South of the city centre lied Capitol Hill, where you will find the major institutions of national government, including the Temple of Justice and the Executive Mansion are located.

Further east down the peninsula is the Sinkor section of Monrovia. Originally a suburban residential district, today Sinkor acts as Monrovia's bustling mid-town, hosting many diplomatic missions, as well as major hotels, businesses, and several residential neighbourhoods, including informal communities such as Plumkor, Jorkpentown, Lakpazee, and Fiamah.

ABIDJAN , IVORY COAST

Abidjan (*AB-ih-JAHN*, French:[abidʒã]) is the economic capital of <u>Ivory Coast</u> and one of the most populous French-speaking cities in Africa. According to the 2014 census, Abidjan's population was 4.7 million, which is 20 percent of the overall population of the country, and this also makes it the sixth most populous city proper in Africa, after Lagos, Cairo Kinshasa, Dar es Salaam, and Johannesburg. A cultural crossroads of West Africa, Abidjan has been characterized today by a high level of industrialization and urbanization.

The city expanded quickly after the construction of a new wharf in 1931, followed by its designation as the capital city of the then-French colony in 1933. Abidjan remained the capital of Côte d'Ivoire after its independence from France in 1960. The completion of the <u>Vridi Canal</u> in the year of 1951 enabled Abidjan to become an important seaport. In 1983, the city Yamoussoukro was designated as the official political capital of Côte d'Ivoire. However, almost all of the political institutions and foreign embassies continue to be located in Abidjan.

Because Abidjan is also the largest city in the country and the centre of its economic activity, it has officially been designated also as the "economic capital" of their country.

The <u>Abidjan District</u>, which encompasses the city and some of its suburbs, is one of the 14 districts of Côte d'Ivoire. Abidjan lies on the south-east coast of the country, on the Gulf of Guinea. The city is located on the Ébrié Lagoon.

The business district, Le Plateau, is the centre of the city, along with <u>Cocody Deux Plateaux</u> (the city's wealthiest neighbourhood and a hub for diplomats), and Adjamé, a slum on the north shore of the lagoon. Treichville and Marcory lie to the south, Attecoube, Locodjro, Abobo Doume and Yopougon to the west, and Lie Boulay is located in the middle of the lagoon.

The business district, Le Plateau, is the centre of the city, along with Cocody, Deux Plateaux (the city's wealthiest neighbourhood and a hub for diplomats), Lie Boulay is located in the middle of the lagoon. Further south lies Port Bouët, home to the airport and main seaport. Abidjan is located at 5°25′ North, 4°2′.

Abidjan was originally a small <u>Atchan fishing</u> village. In 1896, following a series of deadly yellow fever epidemics, French colonists who had settled in <u>Grand Bassam</u> decided to move to a safer place and in 1898 chose the current location of Abidjan. In 1903 it officially became a town. The settlers were followed by the colonial government, created in 1899. But then nearby Bingerville became the capital of the French colony, from 1900 until 1934.

The future Abidjan, situated on the edge of the *lagoon n'doupé* ("the lagoon in hot water"), offered more land and greater opportunities for trade expansion.

TUNIS, TUNISIA

Tunis (Arabic: *Tūnis*) is the capital and the largest city in Tunisia. The greater metropolitan area of Tunis often referred to as *Grand Tunis*, has some 2,700,000 inhabitants.

Situated on a large Mediterranean Sea gulf (the Gulf of Tunis), behind the Lake of Tunis and the port of La Goulette (Ḥalq il-Wād), the city extends along the coastal plain and the hills that surround it. At its core lies its ancient medina, a World Heritage Site. East of the medina through the Sea Gate (also known as the *Bab el Bhar* and the *Porte de France*) begins the modern city, or Ville Nouvelle, traversed by the grand Avenue Habib Bourguiba (often referred to by popular press and travel guides as "the Tunisian Champs-Élysées"), where the colonial-era buildings provide a clear contrast to smaller, older structure.

Further east by the sea lies the suburbs of Carthage, La Marsa, and Sidi Bou Said. As the capital city of the country, Tunis is the focus of Tunisian political and administrative life; it is also the Centre of the country's commercial and cultural activities. It has two cultural centers, as well as a municipal theatre that is used by international theatre groups and a summer festival, the International Festival of Carthage, which is held in July.

Tunis is the transcription of the Arabic name تونس which can be pronounced as "Tūnus", "Tūnas", or "Tūnis". All three variations were mentioned by the Greek-Syrian geographer al-Rumi Yaqout in his *Mu'jam al-Būldan* (*Dictionary of Countries*).

Different explanations exist for the origin of the name *Tunis*. Some scholars relate it to the Phoenician goddess *Tanith* ('Tanit or Tanut), as many ancient cities were named after patron deities. Some scholars claim that it originated from *Tynes*, which was mentioned by Diodorus Siculus and Polybius in the course of descriptions of a location resembling present-day Al-Kasbah; Tunis's old Berber Bourgade.

Another possibility is that it was derived from the Berber verbal root ens which means "to lie down" or "to pass the night". Given the variations of the precise meaning over time and space, the term *Tunis* can mean "camp at night", "camp", or "stop". There are also some mentions in ancient Roman sources of such names of nearby towns as *Tuniza* currently (ElKala), *Thunusuda* (currently Sidi Meskin), *Thinissut* currently (Bir Bouregba), and *Thunisa* currently (Ras Jebel). As all of these Berber villages were situated on Roman roads, they undoubtedly served as rest-stations or stops.

Tunis was originally a Berber settlement. The existence of the town is attested by sources dating from the 4th century BC situated on a hill, Tunis served as an excellent point from which the coming and going of naval and caravan traffic to and from Carthage could be observed. Tunis was one of the first town in the region to fall under Carthaginian control, and in the centuries that followed Tunis was mentioned in the military history associated with Carthage. Thus, during Agathocles' expedition, which landed at Cape Bon in 310 BC, Tunis changed hands on various occasions.

LUSAKA, ZAMBIA

Lusaka (/luːˈsɑːkə/ *loo-SAH-kə*) is the capital and largest city of Zambia. One of the fastest developing cities in southern Africa, Lusaka is in the southern part of the central plateau at an elevation of about 1,279 meters (4,196 ft.). As of 2010, the city's population was about 1.7 million, while the urban population is 2.4 million. Lusaka is the center of both commerce and government in Zambia and connects to the country's four main highways heading north, south, east and west. English is the official language of the city administration, while Chewa and Bemba are the commonly spoken street languages.

Lusaka was the site of a village named after its Chief Lusaka, which, according to history, was located at Manda Hill, near where Zambia's National Assembly building now stands. In the Nyanja language, *Manda* means a graveyard. The area was expanded by European (mainly British) settlers in 1905 with the building of the railway.

After the federation of Northern and Southern Rhodesia in 1953, it was a center of the independence movement amongst some of the educated elite that led to the creation of the Republic of Zambia. In 1964, Lusaka became the capital of the newly independent Zambia

In recent years, Lusaka has become a popular urban settlement for Zambians and tourists alike. Its central nature and fast-growing infrastructure sector have increased donor confidence and as such Zambians are seeing signs of development in the current form of job creation, housing, etc. Consequently, it is also thought that with proper and effecive economic reforms, Lusaka, as well as Zambia as a whole, will develop considerably. Lusaka is home to a diverse community of foreign nationals, many of whom work in the aid industry as well as diplomats, representatives of religious organizations and some business people.

Zambia's largest institution of learning, the University of Zambia, is based in Lusaka. Other universities and colleges located in Lusaka include University of Lusaka (UNILUS), Zambia Open University (ZAOU), Chainama Hills College, Evelyn Hone College, Zambia Centre for Accountancy Studies University (ZCASU), National Institute of Public Administration (NIPA), Cavendish University, Lusaka Apex Medical University, and DMI-St. Eugene University. Lusaka has some of the finest schools in Zambia, including the American International School of Lusaka, Rhodes *Park School*, the Lusaka International Community School, the French International School, the Italian international School, as well as the Lusaka Islamic Cultural and Educational Foundation (LICEF), along with the Chinese International School, and Baobab College.

Attractions include Lusaka National Museum, the Political Museum, the Zintu Community Museum, the Freedom Statue, the Zambian National Assembly, the Agricultural Society Showgrounds (known for their annual agricultural show), the Moore Pottery Factory, the Lusaka Playhouse theatre, two cinema, a cenotaph, a golf club, the Lusaka Central Sports Club, Kalimba Reptile Park, Monkey Pools and the zoo and botanical gardens of the Munda Wanga Environmental Park.

AFRICAN CITIES

FACT CHECK #4

Victoria Falls

South Africa is a land of cultural diversity and scenic beauty. In Southern Africa, Victoria Falls is the largest curtain of water in the world at over 1,600 m (5.249) wide and 100 m (328 ft.) in height (in high flow Victoria Falls can be un- interrupted).

Size and flow rate of Victoria Falls with Niagara Falls for comparison

Devil Pool

Height in meter and feet:	105 m	360 ft	51 m	167 ft
Width in meters and feet:	1,705 m	5,604 ft	1,203 m	3,947 ft
Flow rate units (vol)	m3/S	cu ft/S	m3/5	cu ft/S
Mean annual flow rate:	1,055	38,430	2,407	85,000
Mean monthly flow - max	3,000	105,944		
min	300	10,594		
10yrs max	6,000	211,833		
Highest recorded flow:	12,000	452,000	6,500	240,000

A naturally formed
Safe Swimming Pool

A famous feature of Victoria Falls is its naturally formed safe swimming pool. When the river flow is at a safe level, usually between the month of September and December, people can swim as close as possible to the edge of the falls without continuing over the edge. This is made possible due to a natural rock wall just below the water and at the very edge of the falls that stops their progress despite the current.

ACCRA, GHANA

Accra, (/əˈkrɑː/ is the capital and largest city of Ghana, covering an area of 225.67 km² (87.13 sq. mi) with an estimated urban population of 2.27 million as of 2012. It is organized into 12 local government districts – 11 municipal districts and the Accra Metropolitan District, which is the only district within the capital to be granted city status. "Accra" usually refers to the Accra Metropolitan Area, which serves as the capital of Ghana, while the district which is within the jurisdiction of the Accra Metropolitan Assembly is distinguished from the rest of the capital as the "City of Accra". In common usage, however, the terms "Accra" and "City of Accra" are used interchangeably.

The intersection of the Lafa stream and Mallam Junction serves as the western border of Accra, the Great Hall of the University of Ghana forms Accra's northern border, while the Nautical College forms the eastern border. The Gulf of Guinea forms the southern border.

Formed from the merger of distinct settlements around British Fort James, Dutch Fort Crêvecoeur (Ussher Fort), and Danish Fort Christiansborg as Jamestown, Ussher town, and Christiansborg respectively, Accra served as the capital of the British Gold Coast between 1877 and 1957 and has since transitioned into a modern metropolis. The capital's architecture reflects this history, ranging from the 19th-century colonial architecture to modern skyscrapers and apartment blocks.

Accra is the Greater Accra Region's economic and hub of administration and serves as the anchor of the larger Greater Accra Metropolitan Area (GAMA), which is inhabited by about 4 million people, making it the thirteenth-largest metropolitan area inside of Africa. Strategic initiatives, such as transportation, are coordinated between the local government authorities, while the Accra Metropolitan Assembly, based in West Ridge, is responsible for the administration of the 60 km (23 sq. mi) City of Accra only.

The central business district of Accra contains the city's main banks and also its department stores as well as an area known as the Ministries, where Ghana's gov't administration is concentrated.

Economic activities include the financial and commercial sectors, fishing and the manufacturer of their processed food, lumber, plywood, textiles, clothing, and chemicals. Tourism is becoming a thriving source of business for those in arts and crafts, historical sites and local travel and tour agents. Oxford Street in the district of Osu has grown to become the hub of business and nightlife in Accra.

In 2010, the Globalization and the World Cities Research Network think tank designated Accra as a Gamma level world city, thus indicating a growing level of international influence and connectedness.

MAPUTO, MOZAMBIQUE

Maputo (in Portuguese its pronounce): [mɐ'putu], officially named **Lourenço Marques** until 1976, is today the capital and most populous city of Mozambique. Located near the southern end of the country, it is positioned within 120 km (75 miles) of the Eswatini and South Africa borders. The city has a population of 1,101,170 (as of 2017) distributed over a land area of 347 km (134 sq.mi). The <u>Maputo metropolitan</u> area also includes the neighbouring city of Matola, with a total population of 2,717,437. Maputo is a port city, with an economy centered on commerce. It is also noted for its vibrant cultural scene and distinctive, eclectic architecture.

Maputo is situated on a large natural bay on the Indian Ocean, near where the rivers <u>Tembe, Mbuluzi, Matola and Infulene converge</u>. The city consists of seven administrative divisions, which are each subdivided into quarters or *bairros*. The city is surrounded by Maputo Province but is administered as a self-contained, separate province since 1998. Maputo City is the geographically smallest and most densely populated province in Mozambique. Maputo is a cosmopolitan city, with Bantu, Portuguese and to a lesser extent, Arabic, Indian and Chinese languages and cultures present.

The area on which Maputo stands was first settled as a fishing village in the 1500s. It was soon named Lourenço Marques, after the navigator of the same name who first explored the area in 1544. The modern city traces its origins to a Portuguese fort established on the site in 1781. A town grew around the fort starting around 1850 and in 1877, it was elevated to city status. In 1898, the colony of Portuguese Mozambique relocated its capital there. In the late 19th and early 20th centuries, Lourenço Marques grew both in population and economic development as a port city.

Upon Mozambican independence in 1975, the city became the national capital and was renamed Maputo. During the Mozambican Civil War, the city's economy was devastated. When the war ended, the FRELIMO government launched a program to revive the city's economy, and to clean up the city by forcibly removing criminals, squatters and undocumented residents. Since then, Maputo's economy has recovered and stability has returned, though crime remains a problem.

Maputo has a number of landmarks, including Independence Square, City Hall, Maputo Fortress, the central market, Tunduru Gardens and Maputo Railway Station. Maputo is known as an aesthetically attractive dilapidated city. With area wide avenues lined by jacaranda and acacia trees, it has earned the nick name *City of Acacias* and the *Pearl of the Indian Ocean*. The city is known for its distinct, eclectic architecture, with much more of Portuguese colonial Neoclassical and Manueline styles alongside modern Art Deco, Bauhaus and Brutalist buildings.

The historic *Baixa de Maputo* district is the downtown area. Maputo has a vibrant cultural scene, with many restaurants, music and performance venues and local film industry. Maputo's economy is centered on its port, through which much of Mozambique's imports and exports are shipped each day. The chief exports include cotton, sugar, chromite, sisal, copra, and hardwood. In addition to trade, the city has a robust manufacturing and service sectors. It also has several colleges and universities located in Maputo, including Pedagogical University, São Tomás University, and Eduardo Mondlan.

LAGOS, NIGERIA

Lagos (/'leɪɡɒs,/ Yoruba: *Èkó*) is a city in the Nigerian state of the same name. The city, with its adjoining conurbation, is the most populous in Nigeria and on the African continent. It is one of the fastest-growing cities in the world and one of the most populous urban areas. Lagos is a major financial centre in Africa; the megacity has the fourth-highest GDP in Africa and houses one of the largest and busiest seaports on the continent.

Lagos initially emerged as a port city that originated on a collection of islands, which are contained in the present-day Local Government Areas (LGAs) of Lagos Island, Etiosa, Amuwo-Odofin, and Apapa. The islands are separated by creeks, fringing the southwest mouth of Lagos Lagoon while being protected from the Atlantic Ocean by barrier islands and long sand spits such as Bar Beach, which stretch up to 100 km (62 mi) east and west of the mouth. Due to rapid urbanization, the city expanded to the west of the lagoon to include areas in the present day Lagos Mainland, Ajeromil felodun and Surulere. This led to the classification of Lagos into two main areas: the Island, which was the initial city of Lagos before it expanded into the area known as the Mainland. This city area was governed directly by the Federal Government through the *Lagos City Council*, until the creation of Lagos State in 1967, which led to the splitting of Lagos city into the present day seven Local Government Areas (LGAs), and an addition of other towns (which now make up 13 LGAs) from the then Western Region, to form the state.

Lagos, the capital of Nigeria since its amalgamation in 1914, went on to become the capital of Lagos State after its creation. However, the state capital was later moved to Ikeja in 1976, and the federal capital moved to Abuja in 1991. Even though Lagos is still widely referred to as a city, the present-day Lagos, also known as "Metropolitan Lagos", and officially as "Lagos Metropolitan Area" is an urban agglomeration or conurbation consisting of 20 LGAs, 32 LCDAs including Ikeja, the state capital of Lagos State. This conurbation makes up 37% of Lagos State's total land area, but houses about 85% of the state's total population.

The exact population of Metropolitan Lagos is disputed. In the 2006 federal census data, the conurbation had a population of about 8 million people. However, the figure was disputed by the Lagos State Government, which later released its population data, putting the population of Lagos Metropolitan Area at approximately 16 million. As of 2015, unofficial figures put the population of "Greater Metropolitan Lagos", which includes Lagos and its surrounding metro area, extending as far as into Ogun State, at approximately 21 million.

.

NBA STYLE BASKETBALL is coming to Africa.

And look for:

AFRICA

LEAGUE
Association

<u>To help keep you up to date on game schedules, scores and more</u>

NBA Style Basketball is coming to Africa. "Basketball Africa League" (Bal). Will kick-off this historic event in March 2020. And major cities describe in this book such as Dakar Senegal and other makes up the majority of the cities hosting these historical games. ABLS2020.COM or <u>AfricaBasketballLeagueSchedule.com</u>, will help you keep up with game schedules, scores, stats and more.

Go to: AfricaBasketBallLeagueSchedule,com or ABLS2020.COM

LIBREVILLE, GABON

Libreville, is the capital and largest city of Gabon, in western central Africa. The city is a port on the Komo River, near the Gulf of Guinea, and a trade centre for a timber region. As of 2013, its census population was 703,904.

The area was inhabited by the Mpongwé tribe long before the French acquired the land in 1839.

American missionaries from New England established a mission in Baraka Gabon, on what is now Libreville in 1842. In 1846, the Brazilian slave ship *L'Elizia*, carrying slaves from the Congo, was captured near Loango by the French navy which was tasked with contributing the British Blockade of Africa. Fifty-two of the freed slaves were resettled on the site of Libreville (French for "Freetown") in 1849. It was the chief port of French Equatorial Africa from 1934 to 1946 and was the central focus of the Battle of Gabon in 1940.

In 1910 French Equator Africa (*Afrique equatorial efrançaise*, AEF) was created, and French companies were allowed to exploit the Middle Congo (modern-day Congo-Brazzaville). It soon became necessary to build a railroad that would connect Brazzaville, the terminus of the river navigation on the Congo River and the Ubangui River, with the Atlantic coast. As rapids make it

Impossible to navigate on the Congo River past Brazzaville and the coastal railroad terminus site had to allow for the construction of a deep-sea port, authorities chose the site of Ponta Negra instead of Libreville as originally envisaged.

Construction of the Congo–Ocean Railway began in 1921, and Libreville was surpassed by the rapid growth of Pointe-Noire, farther down the coast.

Libreville was named in imitation of Freetown and grew only slowly as a trading post and a minor administrative Centre to a population of 32,000 on independence in 1960. It only received its first bank branch when Bank of West Africa (BAO) opened a branch in 1930. Since its independence, the city has grown rapidly and now houses nearly half the national population.

Beach in Libreville

From north to south, the major districts of the city are the residential area Batterie IV, Quartier Louis while it is (known for its nightlife), Mont-Bouët and Nombakélé (an active commercial areas), Glass (the first European settlement in Gabon), Oloumia major industrial area) and Lalala, a residential area. The city's port and train station on the Trans-Gabon Railway line to Franceville lied in Owendo, south of the main built-up area. Inland from these districts lies poorer residential areas. North-west of Equatorial Guinea is where the city stands, labeling the city as a part of north-west Gabon. In terms of the country's surrounding boundaries, north is Cameroon, east is Congo, and south-east is the <u>Democratic Republic of the Congo</u>. It also rides the shores of the South Atlantic Ocean, which is on the country's west coast for reference.

LUANDA, ANGOLA

Luanda, formerly named **São Paulo da Assunção de Luanda**, is the capital and largest city in Angola, It is Angola's primary port, and it's major industrial, cultural and urban centre. Located on Angola's northern coast with the Atlantic Ocean, Luanda is both Angola's chief seaport and its administrative Centre. It is also the capital city of Luanda Province. Luanda and its metropolitan area is the most populous Portuguese-speaking capital city in the world, with over 8 million inhabitants in 2019 (a third of Angola's population).

Among the oldest colonial cities of Africa, it was founded in January 1576 by Portuguese explorer Paulo Dias de Novais, under the name of *São Paulo da Assunção de Loanda*. The city served as the center of the slave trade to Brazil before its prohibition. At the start of the Angolan Civil War in 1975, most of the white Portuguese had left as refugees, principally for Portugal. Luanda's population increased greatly from refugees fleeing the war, but its infrastructure was inadequate to handle the increase. This also caused the exacerbation of slums, or musiques around Luanda. The city is currently undergoing a major reconstruction, with many large developments taking place that will alter its cityscape significantly.

The industries present in the city include the processing of agricultural products, beverage production, and textile, cement, with new car assembly plants, construction materials, plastics, metallurgy, cigarettes, and shoes. The city is also notable as an economic centre for oil, and a refinery is located in the city. Luanda has been considered one of the most expensive cities in the world for expatriates. The inhabitants of Luanda are mostly members of the ethnic group of the Ambundu, but in recent times there has been an increase in the number of the Bakongo and the Ovimbundu. There exists a European population, consisting mainly of Portuguese. Luanda was the main host city for the matches of the <u>2010 African Cup of Nations</u>.

Around one-third of Angolans live in Luanda, 53% of whom live in poverty. Living conditions in Luanda are poor for most of the people, with essential services such as safe drinking water and electricity still in short supply, and severe shortcomings in traffic conditions. On the other hand, luxury constructions for the benefit of the wealthy, minority are booming. Luanda is one of the world's most expensive cities for resident foreigners.

New import tariffs imposed in March 2014 made Luanda even more expensive. As an example, a half-liter tub of vanilla ice-cream at the supermarket was reported to cost US$31. The higher import tariffs applied to hundreds of items, from garlic to cars. The stated aim was to try to diversify the heavily oil-dependent economy and nurture farming and industry, sectors which have remained weak. These tariffs have caused much hardship in a country where the average salary was US$260 per month in 2010, the latest year for which data was available. However, the average salary in the booming oil industry was over 20 times higher at US$5,400 per month.

Manufacturing includes some processed foods, beverages, textiles, cement, and other building materials, plastic products, metal ware, cigarettes, as well as shoes/clothes. Luanda has an excellent natural harbour; the chief exports are coffee, cotton, sugar, diamonds, iron, and salt. The city also has a thriving building industry, an effect of the nationwide economic boom experienced since 2002 when political stability returned with the end of the civil war. Damaged during the <u>Angolan Civil War</u> of 1975–2002, its economic growth has been largely supported by their very own oil extraction undertakings, although great diversification is taking place.

Port of Luanda

Dom João II Avenue, one of the main roads in Luanda

Luanda is the starting point of the Luanda railway that goes east to Malanje. The civil war left the railway non-functional, but the railway has been restored up to Dondo and Malanje.

The port of Luanda serves as the largest port of Angola and connects Angola to the rest of the world. A major expansion of this port is also taking place. In 2014, a new port is being developed at Dande, about 30 km to the north.

Luanda's roads are in a poor state of repair but are currently undergoing an extensive reconstruction process by the government in order to relieve traffic congestion in the city. Major road repairs can be found taking place in nearly every neighbourhood, including a major 6-lane highway connected Luanda to Viana. Public transit is provided by the suburban services of the Luanda Railway, by the public company TCUL, and by a large fleet of privately owned collective taxis as white-blue painted mini-busses called *Candongueiro*.

JOHANNESBURG, SO. AFRICA

Johannesburg, informally known as **Jozi** or **Jo'burg**, is the largest city in South Africa and one of the 50 largest urban areas in the world. It is the provincial capital and largest city of Gauteng, which is the wealthiest province in South Africa. While Johannesburg is not one of South Africa's three capital cities, it is the seat of the Constitutional Court. The city is located in the mineral-rich Witwatersrand range of hills and is the center of a large-scale gold and diamond trade.

The metropolis is an alpha global city as listed by the Globalization and World Cities Research Network. In 2019, the population of the city of Johannesburg was 5,635,127, making it the most populous city in South Africa. In the same year, the population of Johannesburg's urban agglomeration was put at 8,000,000. The land area of the municipal city (1,645 km or 635 sq. mi) is large in comparison with those of other major cities, resulting in a moderate population density of 2,364 per square kilometer (6,120/sq. mi).

The city was established in 1886 following the discovery of gold on what had been a farm. The city is commonly interpreted as the modern-day El Doradodue to the extremely large gold deposit found along the Witwatersrand. Within ten years, the population had grown to 100,000 inhabitants.

A separate city from the late 1970s until 1994, Soweto is now part of Johannesburg. Originally an acronym for "South-Western Townships", Soweto originated as a collection of settlements on the outskirts of Johannesburg, populated mostly by native African workers from the gold mining industry. Soweto, eventually incorporated into Johannesburg, had been separated as a residential area for Blacks, who were not permitted at all to live in the city of Johannesburg. Lenasia is predominantly populated by English-speaking South Africans of Indian descent. These areas were designated as non-white areas in accordance with the segregationist policies of the South African government known as Apartheid.

The main Witwatersrand gold reef was discovered in June 1884 on the farm Vogel Struisfontein by Jan Gerritse Bantjes that triggered the Witwatersrand Gold Rush and the founding of Johannesburg in 1886. The discovery of gold rapidly attracted people to the area, making a wanted name and governmental organization for the area. Jan, Johann, and Johannes were common male names among the Dutch of that time; two men involved in surveying the area for the best location of the city, Christian Johannes Joubert and Johann Rissik, are considered the source of the name by some. Johannes Meyer, the first government official in the area is another possibility. Precise records for the choice of names were lost. Within ten years, the city of Johannesburg included 100,000 people.

In September 1884, the Struben brothers discovered the Confidence Reef on the farm Wilgespruit near present-day Roodepoort, which further boosted excitement over gold prospects. The first gold to be crushed on the Witwatersrand was the gold-bearing rock from the Bantjes mine crushed using the Struben brothers stamp machine. Also, news of the discovery soon reached Kimberley and directors Cecil Rhodes with Sir Joseph Robinson rode up to investigate rumors for themselves. They have guided the Bantjes camp with its tents strung out over several kilometers and stayed with Bantjes for two nights.

In 1884, they purchased the first pure refined gold from Bantjes for £3,000. Incidentally, Bantjes had since 1881 been operating the Kromdraai Gold Mine in the Cradle of Humankind together with his partner Johannes Stephanus Minnaar where they first discovered gold in 1881, and which also offered another kind of discovery - the early ancestors of all mankind. Gold was earlier discovered some 249 miles to the east of today Johannesburg in Barberton. Gold prospectors soon discovered the richer gold reefs of the Witwatersrand offered by Bantjes. Mines near Johannesburg are among the deepest in the world, with some as deep as (13,000 ft.).

Rapid growth, Jameson Raid and the Second Boer War

Like many late 19th-century mining towns, Johannesburg was a rough and disorganized place, populated by white miners from all continents, African tribesmen recruited to perform unskilled mine work, African women beer brewers who cooked for and sold beer to the black migrant workers, a very large number of European prostitutes, gangsters, impoverished Afrikaners, tradesmen, and Zulu "Ama Washa", Zulu men who surprisingly dominated laundry work. As the value of control of the land increased, tensions developed between the Boer-dominated Transvaal government in Pretoria and the British, culminating in the Jameson Raid that ended in the fiasco at Doorknob in January 1896. In the Second Boer War (1899–1902) saw British forces under Field Marshal Frederick Sleigh Roberts, 1st Earl Roberts, occupy the city on 30 May 1900 after a series of battles to the south-west of its then-limits, near present-day Krugersdorp.

In 1917, Johannesburg became the headquarters of the Anglo-American Corporation was founded by Ernest Oppenheimer which ultimately became one of the world's largest corporations, dominating both gold-mining and diamond-mining in South Africa. Major building developments took place in the 1930s, after South Africa went off the gold standard new freeways encouraged massive suburban sprawl to the north of the city. In the late 1960s and early 1970s, tower blocks (including the Carlton Centre and the Southern Life Centre) filled the skyline of the central business district.

"A completely refurbished Soccer City stadium in

Johannesburg hosted the 2010 FIFA World Cup"

DOUALA, CAMEROON

Douala, (German: *Duala*) is the largest city in Cameroon and its economic capital. It is also the capital of Cameroon's Littoral Region. Home to Central Africa's largest port and its major international airport, Douala International Airport (DLA), is the commercial and economic capital of Cameroon and the entire CEMAC region was comprising of Gabon, Congo, Chad, Equatorial Guinea, Central African Republic, and Cameroon. Consequently, it handles most of the country's major exports, such as oil, cocoa, and coffee, timber, metals, and fruits. As of 2018, the city and its surrounding area had an estimated population of 2,768,400.The city sits on the estuary of Wouri River and its climate is tropical.

The first Europeans to visit the area were the Portuguese in about 1472. At the time, the estuary of the Wouri River was known as the Rio dos Camarões (Shrimp River). By 1650, it had become the site of a town formed by immigrants, said to have arrived from Congo, who spoke the Duala language. During the 18th century, it was the center of the transatlantic slave trade.

In 1826, Douala appeared to be made of four different villages located in four specific locations: the village of Deido (Dido), of Akwa, of Njo and Hickory-town (today Bonaberi, located on the other side of Wouri River).

Between the year 1884 and 1895, the city was of a German protectorate. The colonial politics focused on commerce and some exploring of the unoccupied territories. In 1885, Alfred Saker organized the first mission of the British Baptist Church. In the same year, the city known as Kamerun was renamed

Douala and became the capital of the territory until 1902, when the capital was moved to Buéa.

In 1907, the Ministry of Colonies was established and Douala had 23,000 citizens.

After World War I in 1919, the German colonial territories became French and British protectorates. France received a mandate to administer Douala. A treaty was signed with the local chiefs.

From 1940 to 1946, it was the capital of Cameroon. In 1955 the city had over 100,000 inhabitants.

In 1960, Cameroon became independent and it became a federal republic, with its capital in Yaoundé. Douala became the major economic city. In 1972 the federal republic became a unified state. Douala then had a population of around 500,000.

In the 1980s, in Cameroon, the struggle for liberalization and multi-partitism grew. Between May and December 1991, Douala was at the center of the civil disobedience campaign called the ghost town operation (*Villemore*) during which economic activities shut down to make the country ungovernable and to force the government to allow multi-partitism and freedom of expression.

With the arrival of the Portuguese in the 15th century, the area was known as *Rio dos Camarões*. Before coming under German rule in 1884, the town was also known as *Cameroon Town*; thereafter it became Kamerun Stadt ("Cameroon City"), the capital of German Kamerun. It was renamed Douala in 1907 after the name of natives known as Douala Ijaws (Njos), and became part of French Cameroon in 1919. Many of the Ijaw (Njo) natives migrated to the Niger Delta in Nigeria during the Portuguese era.

AFRICAN CITIES
FACT CHECK #5

Most popular sport in Africa.

Soccer in Africa (also popularly known as football) is followed passionately from Morocco on down to South Africa. You'll know when an important soccer match is being played in Africa because the country you are visiting will literally come to a standstill.

Everywhere you go in Africa you'll see young boys kicking around a football. Sometimes it may be made of plastic bags with strings wrapped around it, sometime it will be made up of crumpled papers. As long as it can be kicked, there will be a game.

KINSHASA, CONGO

Kinshasa, (kɪnˈʃɑːsə)   formerly <u>Léopoldville</u> French: *Léopoldville*is the capital and the largest city of the Democratic Republic of the Congo. The city is situated alongside the Congo River.

Once a site of fishing and trading villages, Kinshasa is now a megacity with an estimated population of 11 million or more. It faces Brazzaville, the capital of the neighbouring Republic of the Congo, which can be seen in the distance across the wide Congo River, making them the world's second-closest pair of capital cities after Rome and Vatican City. The city of Kinshasa is also one of the DRC's 26 provinces. Because the administrative boundaries of the city-province cover a vast area, over 90 percent of the city province's land is rural in nature, and the urban area occupies a small but expanding section on the western side.

Kinshasa is Africa's third-largest urban area after Cairo and Lagos. It is also the world's largest Francophone urban area (surpassing Paris in population),with French being the language of government, schools, newspapers, public services, and high-end commerce in the city, while Lingala is used as a *lingua franca*   in   the   street.   Kinshasa   hosted   the   14th Francophonie Summit in October 2012. Residents of Kinshasa are known as *Kinois* (in French and sometimes in English) or Kinshasans (English). The indigenous people of the area include the Humbu and Teke.

71

The city was founded as a trading post by Henry Morton Stanley in 1881.It was named Léopoldville in honor of King Leopold II of the Belgians, who also controlled the Congo Free State, the vast territory that is now the Democratic Republic of the Congo, not as a colony but as private property. The post flourished as the first navigable port on the Congo River above Livingstone Falls, a series of rapids over 300 kilometers (190 miles) below Leopoldville. At first, all goods arriving by sea or being sent by sea had to be carried by porters between Léopoldville and Matadi, the port below the rapids and 150 km (93 mi) from the coast. The completion of the Matadi-Kinshasa portage railway, in 1898, provided an alternative route around the rapids and sparked the rapid development of Léopoldville. In 1914, a pipeline was installed so that crude oil could be transported from Matadi to the upriver steamers in Leopoldville. By 1923, the city was elevated to capital of the Belgian Congo, replacing the town of Boma in the Congo estuary. The town, nicknamed "Léo" or "Leopold", became a commercial Centre and grew rapidly during the colonial period.

Monument to Lumumba and the Tower of Limete.

After gaining its independence on 06/301960, following riots in 1959, the Republic of the Congo elected its first Prime Minister Patrice Lumumba. Lumumba's perceived pro-Soviet leanings were viewed as a threat by Western interests. This being the height of the Cold War, the U.S. and Belgium did not want to lose control of the strategic wealth of the Congo, in particular, its uranium. Less than a year after Lumumba's election, the Belgians and the U.S. bought the support of his Congolese rivals and set in motion the events that culminated in Lumumba's assassination. In 1965, with the help of the U.S. and Belgium, <u>Joseph-Désiré Mobutu</u> seized power in the Congo. He initiated a policy of "Authenticity" the names of people and places in the country. In 1966, Léopoldville has renamed *Kinshasa*, for a village named Kinshasa that once stood near the site, today Kinshasa (commune). The city grew rapidly under Mobutu, drawing people from across the country that came in search of their fortunes or to escape ethnic strife elsewhere, thus adding to the many ethnicities and languages already found there.

In the 1990s, a rebel uprising began, which, by 1997, had brought down the regime of Mobutu.Kinshasa suffered greatly from Mobutu's excesses, mass corruption, nepotism and the civil war that led to his downfall. Nevertheless, it is still a major cultural and intellectual Centre for Central Africa, with a flourishing community of musicians and artists. It is also the country's major industrial Centre, processing many of the natural products brought from the interior. The city has recently had to fend off rioting soldiers, who were protesting the government's failure to pay them.

Joseph Kabila, president of the Democratic Republic of the Congo since 2001, is not overly popular in Kinshasa Violence broke out following the announcement of Kabila's victory in the contested election of 2006; the European Union deployed troops (EUFOR RD Congo) to join the UN force in the city. The announcement in 2016 that a new election would be delayed two years led to large protests in September and in December which involved barricades in the streets and left dozens of people dead. Schools and businesses were closed down.

Down at the banks of the Congo River, Kinshasa is a city of sharp contrasts, with affluent residential and commercial areas and three universities alongside sprawling slums. It is located along the south bank of the Congo River, downstream on the Pool Malebo and directly opposite the city of Brazzaville, capital of the Republic of the Congo. The Congo River is the second-longest river in Africa after the Nile and has the continent's greatest discharge. As a waterway it provides a means of transport for much of the Congo basin; it is navigable for large river barges between Kinshasa and Kisangani, and many of its tributaries are also navigable. The river is an important source of hydroelectric power and downstream from Kinshasa; it has the potential to generate power equivalent to the usage of roughly half of Africa's population.

WINDHOEK, NAMIBIA

Windhoek, (/wɪndhʊk/) is the capital and largest city of the Republic of Namibia. It is located in central Namibia in the *Khomas Highland* plateau area, at around 1,700 meters (5,600 ft.) above sea level, almost exactly at the country's geographical Centre. The population of Windhoek in 2011 was 325,858, growing continually due to an influx from all over Namibia. South of the city, the sprawling Heroes' Acre war memorial commemorates Namibia's 1990 independence. On a hilltop in the city Centre are the 1890s Alte Feste, a former military headquarters with historical exhibits, and Independence Memorial Museum. Colonial influences are visible in nearby buildings like the sandstone Lutheran Christus Church.

The city developed at the site of a permanent hot spring known to the indigenous pastoral communities. It developed rapidly after Jonker Afrikaner, Captain of the Orlam, settled here in 1840 and built a stone church for his community. In the decades following, multiple wars and armed hostilities resulted in the neglect and destruction of the new settlement. Windhoek was founded again a second time in the year 1890 by Imperial German Army Major Curt von François when the territory was colonized by the German Empire.

Windhoek is the social, economic, political, and cultural centre of the country, nearly every Namibian national enterprise, governmental body, educational and cultural centre is located.

Theories vary on how the place got its modern name of Windhoek. Most believe it is derived from the Afrikaans word *wind-hoek* (wind corner). Another theory suggests that Captain Jonker Afrikaner named Windhoek after the Winterhoek Mountains at Tulbagh in South Africa, where his ancestors had lived. The first known mention of the name *Windhoek* was in a letter from Jonker Afrikaner to Joseph Tindall, dated 12 August 1844.

In 1840 Jonker Afrikaner established an Orlam settlement at Windhoek. He and his followers stayed near one of the main hot springs, located in the present-day Klein Windhoek suburb. He built a stone church that held 500 people; it was also used as a school. Two Rhenish missionaries, Carl Hugo Hahn and Franz Heinrich Kleinschmidt, started working there in late 1842. Two years later they were driven out by two Methodist Wesleyans, Richard Haddy, and Joseph Tindall. Gardens were laid out and for a while, Windhoek prospered. Wars between the Nama and Herero peoples eventually destroyed the settlement. After a long absence, Hahn visited Windhoek again in 1873 and was dismayed to see that nothing remained of the town's former prosperity. In June 1885, a Swiss botanist found only jackals and starving guinea fowl amongst neglected fruit trees.

Sanderburg, one of the three castles of Windhoek

In 1878, Britain annexed Walvis Bay and incorporated it into the Cape of Good Hope colony in 1884, but Britain did not extend its influence into the interior. A request by merchants from Luderitzbucht resulted in the declaration of a German protectorate over what was called German Southwest Africa in 1884. The borders of the German colony were determined in 1890 and Germany sent a protective corps, under Major Curt von François,the *Schutztruppe*, was to maintain order. Von François position his garrison at Windhoek, which was strategically situated as a buffer between the Nama and Herero peoples. The twelve strong springs provided water for the cultivation of produce and grains.

Colonial Windhoek was founded on 18 October 1890, when von François fixed the foundation stone of the fort, which is now known as Alte Feste (Old Fortress). After 1907, development accelerated as many of the indigenous people migrated from the countryside to the growing town to seek work. More European settlers arrived from Germany and South Africa. Businesses started being erected on the streets of Kaiser (presently Independence Avenue), and along the dominant mountain ridge over the city. At this time, Windhoek's three castles, Heinitzburg, Sanderburg, and including Schwerinsburg, were built.

South African administration after World War 1

The German colonial era came to an end during World War I when South African troops occupied Windhoek in May 1915 on behalf of the British Empire. For the next five years, a South African military government administered Southwest Africa. It was assigned to the United Kingdom as a mandate territory by the newly formed League of Nations, and South Africa administered it. Development of the city of Windhoek and the nation later to be known as Namibia came to a virtual standstill. After World War II, Windhoek's development gradually gained momentum, as more capital became available to improve the area's economy.

After 1955, large public projects were undertaken, such as the building of new schools and hospitals, tarring of the city's roads (a project begun in 1928 with Kaiser Street), and the building of dams and pipelines to stabilize the water supply. The city introduced the world's first potable re-use plant in 1958, treating recycled sewage and sending it directly into the town's water supply. On 1st of October 1966, the then Administrator of South West Africa granted Windhoek the coat of arms, which was registered on 2 October 1970 with the South African Bureau of Heraldry. Initially, a stylized aloe was the principal emblem, but this was amended to a natural aloe on 15 September 1972. The Coat of Arms is described as "a Windhoek aloe with a raceme of three flowers on an island. Crest: A mural crown of Motto: SUUM CUIQUE (To every man his own)".

Harare, Zimbabwe

Harare is the capital of Zimbabwe. On the very edge of the landscaped Harare Gardens, the National Gallery of Zimbabwe has a very large collection of African contemporary art and traditional pieces like baskets, textiles, jewelry and musical instruments. The unusual granite formation Epworth Balancing Rocks is southeast of the city. Wildlife such as zebras and giraffes roam Mukuvisi Woodlands, which has bike paths and a bird park. The city proper has an area of 960.6 km (371 mi) and along with an estimated population of 1,606,000 in 2009, with 2,800,000 in its metropolitan area in 2006. Situated just inside of the north-eastern part in Zimbabwe on the country's Mashonaland region, Harare which incorporates the municipalities of Chitungwiza and Epworth, wherein lied the metropolitan province. The city sits on a plateau at an elevation of 1,483 meters (4,865 ft.) above sea level and its climate falls into the subtropical highland category.

The city was founded in 1890 by the Pioneer Column, a small military force of the British South Africa Company, and named Ft. Salisbury after the UK Prime Minister Lord Salisbury. Company administrators demarcated the city and ran it until Southern Rhodesia achieved responsible government in 1923. Salisbury was thereafter the seat of the Southern Rhodesian (later Rhodesian) government and, between the years 1953-63, the capital of the Central African Federation. It retained the name Salisbury until 1982 when it was renamed Harare on the second anniversary of Zimbabwean independence from the United Kingdom.

The Pioneer Column, a military volunteer force of settlers organized by Cecil Rhodes, founded the city on 12 September 1890 as a fort. They originally named the city Fort Salisbury after the 3rd Marquess of Salisbury, then-Prime Minister of the United Kingdom, and it subsequently became known simply as Salisbury. The Salisbury Polo Club was formed in 1896. It was declared to be a municipality in 1897 and it became a city in 1935.

The area at the time of the founding of the city was poorly drained and earliest development was on the sloping ground along the left bank of a stream that is now the course of a trunk road (Julius Nyerere Way). The first area to be fully drained was near the head of the stream and was named Causeway as a result. This area is now the site of many of the most important government buildings, including the Senate House and the Office of the Prime Minister, now renamed for the use of the President after the position was abolished in January 1988.

Salisbury was the capital of the self-governing British colony of Southern Rhodesia from 1923, and of the Federation of Rhodesia and Nyasaland from 1953-63. Ian Smith's Rhodesian Front government declared Rhodesia independent from the United Kingdom on 11 November 1965 and proclaimed the Republic of Rhodesia in 1970. Subsequently, the nation became the short-lived state of Zimbabwe Rhodesia, it was not until the 18th of April 1980 that the country was internationally recognized as independent as the Republic of Zimbabwe.

The name of the city was changed to Harare on 18 April 1982, the second anniversary of Zimbabwean independence, taking its name from the village near Harare Kopje of the Shona chief Neharawa, whose nickname was "he who does not sleep". Prior to independence, "Harare" was the name of the black residential area now known as Mbare.

Economic difficulties and hyperinflation (1999–2008)
In the early twenty-first century, Harare has been adversely affected by the political and economic crisis that is currently plaguing Zimbabwe, after the contested 2002 presidential election and 2005 parliamentary elections. The elected council

was replaced by a government-appointed commission for alleged inefficiency, but essential services such as rubbish collection and street repairs have rapidly worsened, and are now virtually non-existent. In May 2006, the Zimbabwean newspaper the *Financial Gazette* described the city in an editorial as a "sunshine city-turned-sewage farm". In 2009, Harare was voted to be the toughest city to live in according to the Economist Intelligence Unit's livability poll. The situation was unchanged in 2011, according to the same poll, which is based on stability, healthcare, culture and environment, education, opportunity and infrastructure.

Operation Murambasvina

In May 2005, the Zimbabwean government demolished shanties and backyard cottages in Harare, Epworth and the other cities in the country in Operation Murambatsvina ("Drive out Trash"). It was widely alleged that the true purpose of the campaign was to punish the urban poor for supporting the opposition Movement for Democratic Change and to reduce the likelihood of mass action against the government by driving people out of the cities. The government claimed it was necessitated by a rise in criminality and disease. This was followed by Operation Garikayi/Hlalani Kuhle (Operation "Better Living") a year later which consisted of building concrete housing of poor quality.

In late-March 2010, Harare's Join City Tower was finally opened after fourteen years of delayed construction, marketed as *Harare's new Pride*. Initially, uptake of space in the tower was low, with office occupancy at only 3% in October 2011. By May 2013, office occupancy had risen to around half, with all the retail space occupied. Recently, Harare has been on a comeback in economic, urban development and social service.

AFRICAN CITIES
FACT CHECK #6

Most of the world's greatest treasures and wonders of
The world are found on the continent of Africa; such as the
pyramids, the Hanging Church, Saladin's Citadel, and the
Virgin Mar's Tree. The sphinx and the Heliopolis are on
the continent of Africa and two of the most highly visited
sites on the continent of Africa; a land where tribal, wild
jungles and urban life coexist in an amazing ecosystem.

Taking a look back WHEN....

Some years ago Nick Cannon expressed his disdain for movies such as "Django Unchained" and "12 Years a Slave," saying he's tired of seeing Black people portrayed as slaves on film. Recognizing that African people's history started prior to being enslaved, the actor tweeted that he would like to see Blacks portrayed as kings and queens in films instead.

"Why don't they make movies about our African Kings & Queens? #OurHistory. I would love to see a film about Akhenaton and his beautiful wife Queen Nefertiti or Cetewayo, a King who was a war hero.

To learn more about Nick Cannon plans to start development of his "New Hollywood Trend' film of Black kings and queens, Starring black people.

Email us at:YoursByPopularDemand@gmail.com *(free info)*

KINGS...

Taharqa

Taharqa, is probably one of the most famous rulers of Napata Kush, reigning from 690 to 664 B.C. At 16, this great Nubian king led his armies against the invading Assyrians in defense of his ally, Israel. This action earned him a place in the Bible (Isaiah 37:9) – (2 Kings 19:9).

During his 25-year rule, Taharqa controlled the largest empire in Ancient Africa. His power was equaled only by the Assyrians. These two forces were in constant conflict, but despite continuous warfare, Taharqa was able to initiate a building program throughout his empire, which was overwhelming in scope. The number and majesty of his building projects were legendary, with the greatest being the temple at Gebel Barkla in the Sudan. The temple was carved from rock and decorated with images of Taharqa over 100 feet high.

Although Taharqa's reign was filled with conflict with the Assyrians, it was also a prosperous renaissance period in Egypt and Kush. When Taharqa was about 20 years old, he participated in a historic battle with the Assyrian emperor Sennacherib at Eltekeh. According to the Hebrew Bible, at Hezekiah's request, Taharqa and the Egyptian/Kushite army managed to stall the Assyrian advance on Jerusalem, with Sennacherib eventually abandoning the siege due to the loss of 185,000 soldiers at the hand of the Lord according to Biblical account.

The might of Taharqa's military forces was established at Eltekeh, leading to a period of peace in Egypt. During this period of peace and prosperity, the empire flourished. In the sixth year of Taharqa's reign, prosperity was also aided by abundant rainfall and a large harvest. Taharqa took full advantage of the lull in fighting and abundant harvest. He restored existing temples, built new ones, and built the largest pyramid in the Napatan region. Particularly impressive were his additions to the Temple at Karnak, new temple at Kawa, and temples at Jebel Barka.

King Ramesses II, also referred to as Ramesses the Great, was the third Egyptian pharaoh of the 19th dynasty. He reigned from 1279 to 1213 B.C. He is often regarded as the greatest, most celebrated, and most powerful pharaoh of the Egyptian Empire. His successors and later Egyptians called him the "Great Ancestor." Ramesses II led several military expeditions into the Levant, reasserting Egyptian control over Canaan. He also led expeditions south into Nubia, commemorated in inscriptions at the temples at Beit el-Wali and Gerf Hussein.

At age 14, Ramesses was appointed prince regent by his father Seti I. He is believed to have taken the throne in his late teens and is known to have ruled Egypt for 66 years and 2 months, according to Egypt's contemporary historical records. One account reports he lived to be 99 years old.

Shaka, king of the Zulus, was born in 1787, the son of Zulu Chief Senzangakhona and his wife Nandi. When Shaka was 26, his father died and left the throne to a son, Sijuana. Shaka ambushed and killed Sijuana, taking leadership of the Zulus. He came to power around 1818.

A strong leader and military innovator, Shaka is noted for revolutionizing 19th century Bantu warfare by first grouping regiments by age and training his men to use standardized weapons and special tactics.

He invented the "assegai," a short stabbing spear, and marched his regiments in tight formation, using large shields to fend off the enemies throwing spears. Over the years, Shaka's troops earned such a reputation that many enemies would flee at the sight of them.

As Shaka became more respected by his people, he was able to spread his ideas with greater ease. Because of his background as a soldier, Shaka taught the Zulus that the most effective way of becoming most powerful quickly was by conquering and controlling other tribes. His teachings greatly influenced the social outlook of the Zulu people. The Zulu tribe soon developed a warrior outlook, which Shaka turned to his advantage.

Shaka's hegemony was primarily based on military might, smashing rivals and incorporating scattered remnants into his own army. He added to this with a mixture of diplomacy and patronage, incorporating friendly chieftains, including Zihlandlo of the Mkhize, Jobe of the Sithole, and Mathubane of the Thuli. These peoples were never defeated in battle by the Zulu; they did not have to be. Shaka won them over by subtler tactics, such as patronage and reward.

With cunning and confidence as his tools, Shaka built a small Zulu tribe into a powerful nation of more than a million people and united all tribes in South Africa against European colonial rule. The Zulu nation continued to use Shaka's innovations in wars after his death.

King Mansa Musa I, (Emperor Moses) was an important Malian king, ruling from 1312 to 1337 and expanding the Mali influence over the Niger city-states of Timbuktu, Gao, and DjennE. Musa ruled the Mali Empire and was estimated to have been worth the equivalent of $400 billion in today's currency, which makes him the richest man to ever walk this earth. The emperor was a master businessman and economist and gained his wealth through Mali's supply of gold, salt, and ivory, the main commodities for most of the world during that time.

Musa maintained a huge army that kept peace and policed the trade routes for his businesses. His armies pushed the borders of Mali from the Atlantic coast in the west; beyond the cities of Timbuktu and Gao in the east; and from the salt mines of Taghaza in the north to the gold mines of

Wangar in the south.Musa was also a major influence on the University of Timbuktu, the world's first university and the major learning institution for not just Africa but the world. Timbuktu became a meeting place of poets, scholars, and artists of Africa and the Middle East. Even after Mali declined, Timbuktu remained the major learning centre of Africa for many years.

The death date of Mansa Musa is highly debated among modern historians and the Arab scholars who recorded the history of Mali. When compared to the reigns of his successors, son Mansa Meghan (recorded rule from 1337 to 1341) and older brother Mansa Sulevman (recorded rule from 1341 to 1360), and Musa's recorded 25 years of rule, the calculated date of death is 1337.Other records declare Musa planned to abdicate the throne to his son Maghan, but he died soon after he returned from Mecca in 1325.

Haile Selassie I (23 July 1892 – 27 August 1975)

Haile Selassie reigned as Conquering Lion of the Tribe of Judah, Elect of God, and Emperor of Ethiopia from 2 November 1930 to 12 September 1974, with a brief, but significant break in that long reign due to an Italian invasion that placed Italy's king as Ethiopia's emperor from 9 May 1936 to 5 May 1941. Although Hailie Selassie was ultimately deposed and is thus the last official Emperor of Ethiopia, his renowned remains significant. This man who claimed descent from King Solomon and the Queen of Sheba is today revered by anywhere from 200,000 to 800,000 members of the Rastafari movement as the returned messiah of the Bible, God incarnate!

Hannibal

Readers may want to research on the black features of the Phoenicians, of their Carthaginian descendants and of Hannibal himself to be able to grasp the essence of this writing.

In 3422 of the African era (-814), it is led by Queen Dido-Elissar that the primordial Blacks on the Middle East (Phoenicians) founded the brilliant civilization of Carthage in present-day Tunisia. Through their very strong commercial activity, the Carthaginian's conquered the Maghreb and Libya, southern Spain, as well as Sicily, Sardinia, Corsica, and the Balearic islands. The relations between the Republic of Carthage and the Roman Empire are generally peaceful before the escalation towards a conflict that would begin in-264

At the Origins of Carthaginian-Roman Conflict

In -281, Italian mercenaries took the port Messana in Sicily near mainland Italy. They managed to assert their authority thanks to the military support of the Carthaginians who occupied the greater part of Sicily. Refusing then the African authority, the mercenaries called upon Rome to help dislodge Carthage from Messana. Rome, unwilling to see the Carthaginian influence so close to its territory, decided to answer the call, with the objective of taking back the whole Sicily.

This was the beginning of the first Punic war that would last 23 years, which took place on 2 continents, made hundreds of thousands of deaths, decimated militarily and economically Carthage, and saw the defeated African republic lose Sicily, Sardinia, the Corsica, and pay reparations to Rome.

It is in this context of defeats that General Hamilcar Barca restored a bit of honour by conquering the north-east of Spain. Barca is behind the name of the city of Barcelona. The Barca family – descended from Queen Dido-Elissar – imposed thanks to its military prowess, its influence on Carthage. Hamilcar, bruised by this lost war, made his son Hannibal swear, during a ritual sacrificing an animal, to consider Rome as an eternal enemy and to annihilate the European empire one day.

The emergence of Hannibal

Born in -247, Chenu Bechola Barca already used to accompany his father Hamilcar on the battlefields as a child. His name Hannibal means "he who has the favours of Baal (God)". At 25, he took the family patriotic torch on the death of his brother-in-law Hadrusbal the Fair.

Against the advice of the Carthaginian authorities, Hannibal attacked Saguntum, an ally of Rome. The empire reacted strongly by sending a delegation to intimidate Carthage once again economically stable. The Carthaginian senators in their magnificent palace refused to publicly reject the act of Hannibal. This was the beginning of the second Punic War.

The African lightning that crossed Europe

With an army of 15,000 men including nearly 13,000 Blacks, Hannibal defeated the hostile tribes one by one and arrived at the Franco-Spanish border. In front of him stood the Pyrenees massif 7000 men exhausted by the task desert the ranks, the African general crossed the mountains and reached the Rhone. He crossed the river with his little elephants from Africa and India without losing one. The news of the crossing of this difficult terrain iced the Roman authorities with disbelief. Hannibal continued his irresistible advance thanks to the thousands of new men who have joined his army.

He arrived at the foot of the Alps and climbed the mountain range. His men were dying by thousands falling into ravines, killed by hostile tribes, by the cold in this winter season. With incredible courage, 22,000 men amongst which 12,000 Africans, still managed to reach Italy after 15 days of alpine hell. The Franco-Italian massif cost the African General half of his troops.

Battles against the Romans

The Italian general Scipio knows the gigantic damage caused by the Alps to the troops of Hannibal. So, it is with confidence that he waited with his great army for the first battle. Scipio was defeated and had to be ex-filtrated by his son to escape death. Hannibal continued his inexorable advance. General Simpronius was waiting for him.

The Carthaginians attacked the Roman troops by surprise and pretended to be defeated and run away. Simpronius and his boiling temper known from Hannibal pursued the Carthaginians and fell in an ambush. The ill-prepared Romans were encircled. The African hell in the European cold is unleashed on them. Hannibal's elephants behaved

96

like lions, the killings were horrible, those who managed to escape were victims of the cold. The victory of Lake Trebbia resounded like a thunderclap in Rome.

60,000 Gaulics joined the army of Hannibal, subjugated by his military genius. He crossed the swamps and got an infection in the eye, which caused him to lose sight partially. He was waiting for the new elected general Flaminius in a trap. He has hidden some of his troops on the sides and faced the Romans who charged. Carthaginian troops appeared and encircled them 50,000 Romans were slaughtered in few hours, Flaminius was killed it was carnage. The road to Rome was then a widespread panic.

The Romans prayed incessantly, destroyed their bridges, burnt their fields, and took shelter in wooden fortifications. Faced with Roman authorities hesitant to attack, Hannibal conquered city after city. The Romans encircled him in Capua. He ordered to attach wood to the horns of 2000 cows and in the middle of the night, set fire on these wood pieces. The cows frightened ran in one direction, making the Romans believe – seeing the fire in motion – which the Carthaginians were running away. They pursued them, abandoning a control post in the city by which Hannibal and his men escaped. Rome is enraged at this new setback.

The Romans finally decided to confront the Africans in Cannae. 80 Romans faced the 40,000 men of Hannibal's army. The battle began, and the Carthaginians managed to sink the Romans to the middle. It was an encirclement and butchery. About 70,000 Romans were killed against 6,000 Carthaginians and their allies. As always, Hannibal offered dignified burials to the corpse of high-ranking enemies. Relative and very African humanity which characterizes him in all circumstances, astonished. In the city of Rome, it is the feeling of the end of the world that is so imminent that the government prohibited incessant tears.

A certain status quo settled for 15 years with minor battles. Hannibal took control of many ports and sent his brother Mago to inform Carthage of his victories. Carthage refused to send sufficient help to attack the city of Rome in spite of Hannibal begging.

The re-conquest of the Romans

Scipio, son of General Scipio had exfiltrated his father, attacked the Carthaginians" rear possessions Spain and Hanno Barca died during the fighting against the Romans. Carthage suffered defeats and Hannibal left Italy economically devastated to return to protect his country. After the failure of the negotiations with Scipio, the decisive battle started in Zama. The Carthaginians lost it. This was the end of the Second Punic War. Carthage capitulated and suffered sanctions. Hannibal became Head of Republic and restored Carthage's economy to the extent of increasing the Romans' worries. His presence made the senators, who were fearing retaliation, anxious. Hannibal was forced to flee.

The end of Hannibal and Carthage

The Regent left for exile in Tyre, Lebanon, the home country of the Phoenicians. He plotted to overthrow Rome again without success. Tracked, he went to Armenia where he founded a city, then in Crete were tired of his life of a fugitive, he committed suicide by poisoning. He was 64 years old.

The renewed economic power of Carthage and the omnipresent memory of Hannibal's victories irritated Rome, which provoked Carthage in a war. After only 3 years of resistance, the besieged capital surrendered a victim of hunger. The 50,000 Carthaginian survivors were sold and made slaves. Magnificent buildings were destroyed. The Romans set the city on fire for 70 days. The African Republic died in 147 BC after almost 7 centuries of existence.

Through his countless military exploits including Cannae and Lake Trebia, his resilience under all circumstances, his incredible military expertise, Hannibal is considered today as one of the greatest army generals in human history. His war science is still being taught in military schools in the West nowadays. Had Darthage not refused to send him military support, he would have probably won. With his feats, Ancestor Chenu Bechola Barca is compared in Black history to Djehuty-Mesu (Thutmosis Ill) and Ramesu Maryimana (Ramses ll).

Akhenaten (/ˌækəˈnɑːtən/); also spelled **Echnaton,**

Akhenaton, Ikhnaton, and **Khuenaten**; meaning "Effective for Aten"), known before the fifth year of his reign as **Amenhotep IV** (sometimes given its Greek form, *Amenophis IV*, and meaning "Amun Is Satisfied"), was an ancient Egyptian pharaoh of the 18th Dynasty who ruled for 17 years and died perhaps in 1336 BC or 1334 BC. He is noted for abandoning traditional Egyptian polytheism and introducing worship centered on the Aten, which is sometimes described as monolatristic, henotheistic, or even quasi-monotheistic. An early inscription likens the Aten to the sun as compared to stars, and later official language avoids calling the Aten a god, giving the solar deity a status above mere gods.

Akhenaten tried to shift his culture from Egypt's traditional religion, but the shifts were not widely accepted. After his death, his monuments were dismantled and hidden, his statues were destroyed, and his name excluded from the king lists. Traditional religious practice was gradually restored, and when some dozen years later rulers without clear rights of succession from the 18th Dynasty founded a new dynasty, they discredited Akhenaten and his immediate successors, referring to himself as "the enemy" or "that criminal" in archival records.

He was all but lost from history until the discovery during the 19th century of the site of Akhenaten, the city he built and designed for the worship of Aten, at Amarna. Early excavations at Amarna by Flinders Petrie sparked interest in the enigmatic pharaoh, and a mummy found in the tomb KV55, which was unearthed in 1907 in a dig led by Edward R. Ayrton, is likely that of Akhenaten. DNA analysis has determined that the man buried in KV55 is the father of King Tutankhamun,
but its identification as Akhenaten has been questioned.

Modern interest in Akhenaten and his queen Nefertiti comes partly from his connection with Tutankhamun (even though Tutankhamun's mother was not Nefertiti, but a woman named by archaeologists (The Younger Lady), partly from the unique style and high quality of the pictorial arts he patronized, and partly from ongoing interest in the religion, he attempted to establish.

The future Akhenaten was a younger son of Amenhotep III and Chief Queen Tiye. The eldest son Crown Prince Thutmose was recognized as the heir of Amenhotep III but he died relatively young and the next in line for the throne was a prince named Amenhotep.

There is much controversy around whether Amenhotep IV succeeded to the throne on the death of his father Amenhotep III or whether there was a coregency (lasting as long as 12 years according to some Egyptologists). Current literature by Eric Cline, Nicholas Reeves, Peter Dorman and other scholars comes out strongly against the establishment of a long coregency between the two rulers and in favour of either no coregency or a brief one lasting one to two years at the most.

In February 2014, the Egyptian Ministry for Antiquities announced what it called conclusive evidence that Akhenaten shared power with his father for at least 8 years. The evidence came from the inscriptions found in the Luxor tomb of Vizier Amenhotep-Huy. A team of Spanish archaeologists has been working at this tomb.

During the early years in Thebes, Akhenaten (still known as Amenhotep IV) had several temples erected at Karnak. One of the structures, the Mansion of the Benben (ben-ben), was dedicated to Nefertiti. She is depicted with her daughter Meritaten and in some scenes the princess Meketaten participates as well. In scenes found on the talatat, Nefertiti appears almost twice as often as her husband. She is shown appearing behind her husband the Pharaoh in offering scenes in the role of the queen supporting her husband, but she is also depicted in scenes that would have normally been the prerogative of the king. She is shown smiting the enemy, and captive enemies decorate her throne.

In the fourth year of his reign, Amenhotep IV decided to move the capital to Akhenaten (modern Amarna). In his fifth year, Amenhotep IV officially changed his name to Akhenaten, and Nefertiti was henceforth known as Neferneferuaten-Nefertiti. The name change was a sign of the ever-increasing importance of the cult of the Aten. It changed Egypt's religion from a polytheistic religion to a religion which may have been better described as a monolatry (the depiction of a single god as an object for worship) or henotheism (one god, who is not the only god).

Amenhotep IV and Nefertiti are shown in the window of appearance, with the Aten depicted as the sun disc. In the Theban tomb of Parennefer, Amenhotep IV and Nefertiti are seated on a throne with the sun disk depicted over the king and queen.

Among the latter-known documents referring to Amenhotep IV are two copies of a letter from the Steward of Memphis Apy (or Ipy) to the pharaoh. The documents were found in Gurob and are dated to regnal year 5, the third month of the Growing Season, day 19.

NeferneferuatenNefertiti (/ˌnɛfərˈtiːti/) (c. 1370 – c. 1330 BC)

Nefertiti was an Egyptian queen and the Great Royal Wife of Akhenaten an Egyptian Pharaoh. Nefertiti and her husband were known for a religious revolution, in which they worshipped one god only, Aten, or the sun disc. With her husband, she reigned at what was arguably the wealthiest period of Ancient Egyptian history. Some scholars believe that Nefertiti ruled briefly after her husband's death and before the accession of Tutankhamun, although this identification is a matter of ongoing debate. If Nefertiti did rule as Pharaoh, her reign was marked by the fall of Amarna and relocation of the capital back to the traditional city of Thebes.

Nefertiti had many titles including Hereditary Princess, Great of Praises, Lady of Grace, Sweet of Love, Lady of The Two Lands, Main King's Wife, his beloved; Great King's Wife, His beloved, Lady of all Women; and Mistress of Upper and Lower Egypt. She was made famous by her bust, now in Berlin's Neues Museum. The bust is one of the most copied works from ancient Egypt. It was mostly attributed to the sculptor Thutmose, and it was found in his workshop.

Nefertiti's name, Egyptian *Nfr.t-jy.tj*, can be translated as "The Beautiful Woman has come". Nefertiti's parentage is not known with certainty, but one often cited theory is that she was the daughter of Ay, later to be pharaoh. One major problem of this theory is that neither Ay nor his wife Tey are explicitly called the father and mother of Nefertiti in existing sources. Tey's only connection with her was that she was the "nurse of the great queen" Nefertiti, an unlikely title for a queen's mother. At the same time, no sources exist that directly contradict Ay's fatherhood which is considered likely due to the great influence he wielded during Nefertiti's life and after her death.

To solve this problem, it has been proposed that Ay had another wife before Tey, namely Iuy, whose existence and connection to Ay is suggested by some evidence. According to this theory, Nefertiti was the daughter of Ay and Iuy, but her mother died before her rise to the position of queen, whereupon Ay married Tey, making her Nefertiti's step-mother. This entire, proposal is based on speculation and conjecture, nevertheless.

It has also been proposed that Nefertiti was Akhenaten's full sister, though this is contradicted by her titles which do not include those usually used by the daughters of a Pharaoh. Another theory about her parentage that gained some support identified Nefertiti with the Mitanni princess Tadukhipa, partially based on Nefertiti's name ("The Beautiful Woman has come") which has been interpreted by some scholars as signifying a foreign origin. The exact dates when Nefertiti married Akhenaten and became the king's great royal wife of Egypt are uncertain. Their six known daughters (and estimated years of birth) were:

- Meritaten: No later than year 1, possibly later became Pharaoh Neferneferuaten.

  - If Nefertiti did rule Egypt as Pharaoh, it has been theorized that she would have attempted damage control and may have re-instated the Ancient Egyptian religion and the Amun priests and had Tutankhamun raised in with the traditional gods

  - Archaeologist and Egyptologist Dr Zahi Hawass theorized that Nefertiti returned to Thebes from Amarna to rule as Pharaoh, based on ushabti and other feminine evidence of a female Pharaoh found in Tutankhamun's tomb, as well as evidence of Nefertiti smiting Egypt's enemies which were a duty reserved to kings.

The boundary stelae of years 4 and 5 marks the boundaries of the new city and suggest that the move to the new city of Akhenaten occurred around that time. The new city contained several large open-air temples dedicated to the Aten. Nefertiti and her family would have resided in the Great Royal Palace in the Centre of the city and possibly at the Northern Palace as well. Nefertiti and the rest of the royal family feature prominently in the scenes at the palaces and in the tombs of the nobles. Nefertiti's steward during this time was an official named Meryre II. He would have been in charge of running her household.

Inscriptions in the tombs of Huya and Meryre II dated to Year 12, 2nd month of Peret, Day 8 show a large foreign tribute. The people of Kharu (the north) and Kush (the south) are shown bringing gifts of gold and precious items to Akhenaten and Nefertiti. In the tomb of Meryre II, Nefertiti's steward, the royal couple is shown seated in a kiosk with their six daughters in attendance. This is one of the last times' princess Meketaten is shown alive.

Two representations of Nefertiti that were excavated by Flinders Petrie appear to show Nefertiti in the middle to later part of Akhenaten's reign 'after the exaggerated style of the early years had relaxed somewhat' One is a small piece of limestone and is a preliminary sketch of Nefertiti wearing her distinctive tall crown with carving began around the mouth, chin, ear and tab of the crown. Another is a small inlay head (Petrie Museum Number UC103) modeled from reddish-brown quartzite that was intended to fit into a larger composition.

Meketaten may have died in year 13 or 14. Nefertiti, Akhenaten, and three princesses are shown mourning her. The last dated inscription naming her and Akhenaten comes from a building inscription in the limestone quarry at Dayr Abū Ḥinnis. It dates to year 16 of the king's reign and is also the last dated inscription naming the king.

Queen Cleopatra VII Thea Philopator the Great (Late 69
BC – 12 August 30 BC)

Cleopatra, is the most notable African ruler to be named
"the Great" and a major aspect of modern popular culture.
Her life has been depicted in many plays and films produced
in Europe and America despite her being an Egyptian
pharaoh. Unlike the other women on this list, her descent
comes from the Greco-Macedonian armies of Alexander the

Great that captured Egypt from the Persian Empire nearly three centuries before her life. Her personality and ambition are legendary. She reportedly was introduced to Julius Caesar by being unrolled from a rug. She so captivated him that they had a son nicknamed Little Caesar.

After Julius's assassination, she allied with Mark Antony and appeared on coins as a goddess ("Thea"), while referring to herself as Nea Isis, thereby suggested she was the resurrected form of the goddess Isis. Anticipating al-Gaddafi's megalomania by a couple thousand years, she styled herself as Queen of Kings and her son as King of Kings, but unlike al-Gaddafi, Cleopatra had a much more realistic chance of making this lofty claim a reality. Had he and Antony's forces defeated their rival Octavian at Actium (31 BC), the history of the entire Mediterranean may have been altered fundamentally with Alexandria, rather than Rome being the great superpower of antiquity.

Yet, even though she ultimately failed and her death meant the end of the Egypt of the Pharaohs, her intelligence and cunning in a male-dominated world remain admirable.

Cleopatra knew how to make an entrance.

Cleopatra believed herself to be a living goddess, and she often used clever stagecraft to woo potential allies and reinforce her divine status. A famous example of her flair for the dramatic came in 48 B.C., when Julius Caesar arrived in Alexandria during her feud with her brother Ptolemy XIII. Knowing Ptolemy's forces would thwart her attempts to meet with the Roman general, Cleopatra had herself wrapped in a carpet—some sources say it was a linen sack—and smuggled into his personal quarters. Caesar was dazzled by the sight of the young queen in her royal garb, and the two soon became allies and lovers.

Following the tradition of Macedonian rulers, Cleopatra ruled Egypt and other territories such as Cyprus as an absolute monarch, serving as the sole lawgiver of her kingdom. She was the chief religious authority in her realm, presiding over religious ceremonies that are dedicated to the deities of both the Egyptian and Greek polytheistic faiths. She oversaw the construction of various temples to Egyptian and Greek gods, a synagogue for the Jews in Egypt, and even built as well, the Caesareum of Alexandria dedicated to the cult worship of her patrons and lover Julius Caesar.

Cleopatra was directly involved in the administrative affairs of her domain, tackling crises such as famine by ordering royal granaries to distribute food to the starving populace during a drought at the beginning of her reign. Although the command economy that she managed was more of an ideal than a reality, the government attempted to impose their price controls, tariffs, and state monopolies for certain goods, fixed exchange rates for foreign currencies, and rigid laws forcing peasant farmers to stay in their villages during planting and harvesting seasons. Apparent financial troubles led Cleopatra to debase her coinage, which included silver and bronze currencies but no gold coins like those of some of her distant Ptolemaic predecessors.

Cleopatra's legacy survives in ancient and modern works of art. Roman historiography and Latin poetry produced a generally critical view of the queen that pervaded later Medieval and Renaissance literature. In the visual arts, her ancient depictions include Roman busts, paintings, and sculptures, cameo carvings and glass, Ptolemaic and Roman coinage, and reliefs. In Renaissance and Baroque art she was the subject of many works including operas, paintings, poetry, sculptures, and theatrical dramas. She has become a pop culture icon of Egyptomania since the Victorian era, and in modern times Cleopatra has appeared in the applied and fine arts, burlesque satire, Hollywood films, and brand images for commercial products.

After her suicide, Cleopatra's three surviving children, Cleopatra Selene II, Alexander Helios, and Ptolemy Philadelphos, were sent to Rome with Octavian's sister Octavia the Younger, a former wife of their father, as their guardian. Cleopatra Selene II and Alexander Helios were present in the Roman triumph of Octavian in 29 BC. The fates of Alexander Helios and Ptolemy Philadelphus are unknown after this point. Octavia arranged the betrothal of Cleopatra Selene II to Juba II, son of Juba I, whose North African kingdom of Numidia had been turned into a Roman province in 46 BC by Julius Caesar due to Juba I's support of Pompey.

The emperor Augustus installed Juba II and Cleopatra Selene II, after their wedding in 25 BC, as the new ruler of Mauretania, where they transformed the old Carthaginian city of Iol into their new capital, renamed Caesarea Mauretaniae (modern Cherchell, Algeria). Cleopatra Selene II imported many important scholars, artists, and advisers from her mother's royal court in Alexandria to serve her in Caesarea, now permeated in Hellenistic Greek culture. She also named her son Ptolemy of Mauretania, in honour of their Ptolemaic dynastic heritage.

Cleopatra Selene II died around 5 BC, and when Juba II died in 23/24 AD he was succeeded by his son Ptolemy. However, Ptolemy was eventually executed by the Roman emperor Caligula in 40 AD, perhaps under the pretense that Ptolemy had unlawfully minted his royal coinage and utilized regalia reserved for the Roman emperor. Ptolemy of Mauretania was the last known monarch of the Ptolemaic dynasty, although Queen Zenobia, of the short-lived Palmpeyrene Empire during the Crisis of the Third Century, would claim descent from Cleopatra. A cult dedicated to Cleopatra still existed as late as 373 AD when Petesenufe, an Egyptian scribe of the book of Isis, explained that he "overlaid the figure of Cleopatra with gold."

The Queen of Sheba's visit to Solomon: around 1555

The Queen of Sheba (Hebrew: שְׁבָא מַלְכַּת־) *malkat-šəḇā* in the Hebrew Bible, Koinē, came to Jerusalem "with a very great retinue, with camels bearing spices, and very much gold, and precious stones" (I Kings 10-2) "Never again came such an abundance of spices" (10:10; II Chron. 9:1–9) as those she gave to Solomon. She came "to prove him with hard questions", which Solomon answered to her satisfaction. They exchanged gifts, after which she returned to her land.

The use of the term *ḥiddot* or 'riddles' (I Kings 10:1), an Aramaic loanword whose shape points to a sound shift no earlier than the sixth century B.C., indicates a late origin for the text. Since there is no mention of the fall of Babylon in 539 BC, Martin Noth has held that the Book of Kings received a definitive redaction around 550 BC.

Virtually all modern scholars agree that Sheba was the South Arabian kingdom of Saba, centered on the oasis of Marib in present-day Yemen. Sheba was quite well known in the classical world, and its country was called Arabia Felix. Around the middle of the first millennium B.C., there were Sabaeans also in the Horn of Africa, in the area that later became the realm of Aksum.

There are five places in the Bible where the writer distinguishes *Sheba*, the Yemenite Sabaeans, from *Seba* (the African Sabaeans). In Ps. 72:10 they are mentioned together: "the kings of Sheba and Seba shall offer gifts". This spelling differentiation, however, may be purely fictitious; the indigenous inscriptions make no such difference, and both Yemenite and African Sabaeans are there spelled in the same way.

The alphabetic inscriptions from South Arabia furnish no evidence for women rulers, but Assyrian inscriptions repeatedly mention Arab queens in the north. Queens are well attested in Arabia, though according to Kitchen, not after 690 B.C. Furthermore, Sabaean tribes knew the title of ("high official'). *Makada* or *Makueda*, the personal name of the queen in Ethiopian legend, might be interpreted as a popular rendering of the title. This title may be derived from Ancient Egyptian *m'kit* protectress, housewife"

The queen's visit could have been a trade mission. Early South Arabian trade with Mesopotamia involving wood and spices transported by camels is attested in the early ninth century B.C. and may have begun as early as the tenth.

The ancient Sabaic Awwām Temple, known in folklore as *Maḥram* ("the Sanctuary of") *Bilqīs*, was recently excavated by archaeologists, but no trace of the Queen of Sheba has been discovered so far in the many inscriptions found there. Another Sabean temple, the Barran Temple is also known as the *'Arash Bilqis* ("Throne of Bilqis"), which like the nearby Awam Temple was also dedicated to the god Almaqah, but the connection between the Barran Temple and Sheba has not been established archaeologically either.

Bible stories of the Queen of Sheba and the ships of Ophir served as a basis for legends about the Israelites traveling in the Queen of Sheba's entourage when she returned to her country to bring up her child by Solomon.

Christian scriptures mention a "queen of the South" (Greek: βασίλισσα νότου, Latin: *Regina austri*), who "came from the uttermost parts of the earth", from the extremities of the then known world, to hear the Wisdom of Solomon (Mt. 12:42; Lk. 11:31).

The mystical interpretation of the Song of Songs, which was felt as supplying a literal basis for the speculations of the allegorists, makes its first appearance in Origen, who wrote a voluminous commentary on the Song of Songs. In his commentary, Origen identified the bride of the Song of Songs with the "queen of the South" of the Gospels, i.e. the Queen of Sheba, who is assumed to have been Ethiopian. Others have proposed either the marriage of Solomon with Pharaoh's daughter or his marriage with an Israelite woman, the Shulamite. The former was the favourite opinion of the mystical interpreters to the end of the 18th century; the latter has obtained since its introduction by Good (1803).

114

The Queen of Sheba, from a 15th-century manuscript now at *Staats –*

Solomon and the Queen of Sheba, Giovanni De Min

The bride of Canticles is assumed to have been black due to a passage in Song of Songs 1:5, which the Revised Standard Version (1952) translates as "I am very dark" while the New Revised Standard Version (1989) has "I am black and beautiful".

One legend has it that the Queen of Sheba brought Solomon the same gifts that the Magi later gave to Christ. During the 'Middle Ages, christians sometimes identified the queen of Sheba with the sibyl *Sabba.*

The story of Solomon and the queen was popular among Copts, as shown by fragments of a Coptic legend preserved in a Berlin papyrus. The queen, having been subdued by deceit, gives Solomon a pillar on which all earthly science is inscribed. Solomon sends one of his demons to fetch the pillar from Ethiopia, whence it instantly arrives. In a Coptic poem, queen Yesaba of Cush asks riddles of Solomon.

The fullest and most significant version of the legend appears in the *Kebra Nagast* (Glory of the Kings), the Ethiopian national saga, translated from Arabic in 1322.Here Menelik I is the child of Solomon and *Makeda* (the Ethiopic name of Bilkis) from whom the Ethiopian dynasty claims descent to the present day. While the Abyssinian story offers much greater detail, it omits any mention of the Queen's hairy legs or any other element that might reflect on her unfavourably.

Based on the Gospels of Matthew (12:42) and Luke (11:31), the "queen of the South" is claimed to be the queen of Ethiopia. In those times, King Solomon sought merchants from all over the world, in order to buy materials for the building of the Temple. Among them was Tamrin, great merchant of Queen Makeda of Ethiopia. Having returned to Ethiopia, Tamrin told the queen of the wonderful things he had seen in Jerusalem, and of Solomon's wisdom and generosity, whereupon she decided to visit Solomon. She was warmly welcomed, given a palace for dwelling, and received great gifts every day. Solomon and Makeda spoke with great wisdom, and instructed by him, she converted to Judaism. Before she left, there was a great feast in the king's palace. Makeda stayed in the palace overnight, after Solomon had sworn that he would not do her any harm, while she swore in return that she would not steal from him. As the meals had been spicy, Makeda awoke thirsty at night and went to drink some water, when Solomon appeared, reminding her of her oath. She answered: "Ignore your oath, just let me drink water." That same night, Solomon had a dream about the sun rising over Israel, but being mistreated and despised by the Jews, the sun moved to shine over Ethiopia and Rome (the Byzantine Empire).

Solomon gave Makeda a ring as a token of faith, and then she left. On her way home, she gave birth to a son, whom she named Baina-leḥkem (bin al-ḥakīm), "Son of the Wise Man", later called Menilek). After the boy had grown up in Ethiopia, he went to Jerusalem carrying the ring and was received with great honours. The king and the people tried in vain to persuade him to stay. Solomon gathered his nobles and announced that he would send his first-born son to Ethiopia together with their first-borns. He added that he was expecting a third son, who would marry the king of Rome's daughter and reign over Rome so that the entire world would be ruled by David's descendants. Then Baina-leḥkem was anointed king by Zadok the high priest, and he took the name, David. The first-born nobles who followed him are named, and even today some Ethiopian families claim their ancestry from them. Prior to leaving, the priests' sons had stolen the Ark of the Covenant, after their leader Azaryas had offered a sacrifice as commanded by one God's angel. With much wailing, the procession left Jerusalem on a wind cart lead and carried by the archangel Michael. Having arrived at the Red Sea, Azaryas revealed to the people that the Ark is with them. David prayed to the Ark and the people rejoiced singing, dancing, blowing horns and flutes, and beating drums. The Ark showed its miraculous powers during the crossing of the stormy Sea, and all arrived unscathed. When Solomon learned that the Ark had been stolen, he sent a horseman after the thieves and even gave chase himself, but neither could catch them. Solomon returned to Jerusalem and gave orders to the priests to remain silent about the theft and to place a copy of the Ark in the Temple so that the foreign nations could not say that Israel had lost its fame.

According to some sources, Queen Makeda was part of the dynasty founded by ZaBesi Angabo in 1370 B.C., with her grandfather and father being the last male rulers of the royal line. The family's intended choice to rule Aksum was Makeda's brother, Prince Nourad, but his early death led to her succession to the throne. She apparently ruled the Ethiopian kingdom for more than 50 years.

In the Ethiopian Book of Aksum, Makeda is described as establishing a new capital city at Azeba. Edward Ullendorff holds that *Makeda* is a corruption of Candace, the name or title of several Ethiopian queens from Meroe or Seba. Candace was the name of that queen of the Ethiopians whose chamberlain was converted to Christianity under the preaching of Historians believes that the Solomonic dynasty actually began in 1270 with the emperor Yekuno Amlak, who, with the support of the Ethiopian Church, overthrew the Zagwe Dynasty, which had ruled Ethiopia since sometime during the 10th century. The link to King Solomon provided a strong foundation for Ethiopian national unity. "Ethiopians see their country as God's chosen country, the final resting place that he chose for the Ark – and Sheba and her son were the means by which it came there". Despite the fact that the dynasty officially ended in 1769 with Emperor Iyoas, Ethiopian rulers continued to trace their connection to it, right up to the last 20th-century emperor, Haile Selassie.

According to one tradition, the Ethiopian Jews (Beta Israel, "Falashas") also trace their ancestry to Menelik I, son of King Solomon and the Queen of Sheba. An opinion that appears more historical is that the Falashas descend from those Jews who settled in Egypt after the first exile, and who, upon the fall of the Persian domination (539–333 B.C.) on the borders of the Nile, penetrated into Sudan, whence they went into the western parts of Abyssinia.

Several emperors have stressed the importance of the *Kebra Negast*. One of the first instances of this can be traced in a letter from Prince Kasa (King John IV) to Queen Victoria in 1872.Kasa states, "There is a book called *Kebra Nagast* which contains the law of the whole of Ethiopia, and the names of the shums (governors), churches and provinces are in this book. I pray you will find out who has got this book and send it to me, for in my country my people will not obey my orders without it. Despite the historic importance given to the *KebraNegast,* there is still doubt whether or not the Queen sat on the throne.

According to Josephus (Ant. 8:165–173), the queen of Sheba was the queen of Egypt and Ethiopia and brought to Israel the first specimens of the balsam, which grew in the Holy Land in the historian's time. Josephus (Antiquities 2.5–2.10) represents Cambyses as conquering the capital of Aethiopia and changing its name from Seba to Meroe. Josephus affirms that the Queen of Sheba or Saba came from this region and that it bore the name of Saba before it was known by that of Meroe. There seems also some affinity between the word Saba and the name or title of the kings of the Aethiopians, Sabaco.

The Talmud (BavaBatra 15b) insists that it was not a woman but a kingdom of Sheba (based on varying interpretations of Hebrew *mlkt*) that came to Jerusalem, obviously intended to discredit existing stories about the relations between Solomon and the Queen. Baba Bathra 15b: "Whoever says *malkath Sheba* (I Kings X, 1) means a woman is mistaken; ... it means the kingdom of Sheba" This is explained to mean that she was a woman who was not in her position because of being married to the king but through her own merit.

The most elaborate account of the queen's visit to Solomon is given in the 8th century Targum Sheni to Esther see: (Colloquy of the Queen of Sheba). A hoopoe informed Solomon that the kingdom of Sheba was the only kingdom on earth not subject to him and that its queen was a sun worshiper. He thereupon sent it to Kitor in the land of Sheba with a letter attached to its wing commanding its queen to come to him as a subject. She thereupon sent him all the ships of the sea loaded with precious gifts and 6,000 youths of equal size, all born at the same hour and clothed in purple garments. They carried a letter declaring that she could arrive in Jerusalem within three years although the journey normally took seven years. When the queen arrived and came to Solomon's palace, thinking that the glass floor was a pool of water, she lifted the hem of her dress, uncovering her legs. Solomon informed her of her mistake and reprimanded her for her hairy legs. She asked him three (Targum Sheni to Esther 1:3) or, according to the Midrash (Prov. ii. 6; Yalk. ii. § 1085, Midrash ha-Hefez), more riddles to test his wisdom.

A Yemenite manuscript entitled "Midrash ha-Hefez" (published by S. Schechter in *Folk-Lore,* 1890, pp. 353 et seq.) gives nineteen riddles, most of which are found scattered through the Talmud and the Midrash, which the author of the "Midrash ha-Hefez" attributes to the Queen of Sheba. Most of these riddles are simply Bible questions,

118

some not of a very edifying character. The two that are genuine riddles are: "Without movement, while living, it moves when its head is cut off", and "Produced from the ground, man produces it, while its food is the fruit of the ground". The answer to the former is, "a tree, which, when its top is removed, can be made into a moving ship"; the answer to the latter is, "a wick".

The rabbis who denounce Solomon interpret I Kings 10:13 as meaning that Solomon had criminal intercourse with the Queen of Sheba, the offspring of which was Nebuchadnezzar, who destroyed the Temple (comp. Rashi ad loc.).The Alphabet of Sirach avers that Nebuchadnezzar was the fruit of the union between Solomon and the Queen of Sheba. In the Kabbalah, the Queen of Sheba was considered one of the queens of the demons and is sometimes identified with Lilith, first in the Targum of Job (1:15), and later in the Zohar and the subsequent literature. A Jewish and Arab myth maintains that the Queen was actually jinn, half human and half demon. In Ashkenazi folklore, the figure merged with the popular image of Helen of Troy or the Frau Venus of German mythology. Ashkenazi incantations commonly depict the Queen of Sheba as a seductive dancer. Until recent generations, she was popularly pictured as a snatcher of children and a demonic witch.

I found [there] a woman ruling them, and she has been given of all things, and she has a great throne. I found her and her people prostrating to the sun instead of Allah, and Satan has made their deeds pleasing to them and averted them from [His] way, so they are not guided.

In the above *ayah*, after scouting nearby lands, a bird known as the *hud-hud* (hoopoe) returns to King Solomon relating that the land of Sheba is ruled by a Queen. In a letter, Solomon invites the Queen of Sheba, who like her followers had worshipped the sun, than submit to Allah. She expresses that the letter is noble and asks her chief advisers what action should be taken. They respond by mentioning that her kingdom is known for its might and inclination towards war, however, that the command rests solely with her. In an act suggesting the diplomatic qualities of her leadership, she responds not with brute force, but by sending her ambassadors to present a gift to King Solomon. He refuses the gift, declaring that Allah gives far superior gifts and that the ambassadors are the ones only delighted by the gift.

King Solomon instructs the ambassadors to return to the Queen with a stern message that if he travels to her, he will bring a contingent that she cannot defeat. The Queen then makes plans to visit

119

him at his palace. Before she arrives, King Solomon has her throne moved to his palace with the aid of a scholar of the scripture, who was able to move the throne in the blink of an eye. King Solomon disguises her throne to test her awareness, asking her if it seems familiar. She answers that during her journey to him, her court had informed her that the throne disappeared and since then she and her subjects had made the intention to submit to Allah. King Solomon then explains that Allah is the only god that she should worship, not to be included alongside other false gods that she used to worship. Later the Queen of Sheba is requested to enter a palatial hall. Upon her first view, she mistakes the hall for a lake and raises her skirt to not wet her clothes. King Solomon informs her that is not water rather it is smooth slabs of glass. Recognizing that it was a marvel of construction which she had not seen the likes of before, she declares that in the past she had harmed her own soul but now submits, with King Solomon, to Allah (27:22–44).

Zulu queen. *Born in the 1760s in what is now South Africa; died in 1827; married Zulu chief...Senzangakhona (or Senzangakhoma), around 1787; children: at least one son, Shaka (born around 1787), Zulu chief.*

Nandi, whose name means "a woman of high esteem," was born into the Langeni tribe in the mid-18th century, in what is now South Africa. Around 1787, she had an illicit affair with Senzangakhona, the chief of the Zulu tribe, and gave birth to Shaka, who would later become one of the greatest Zulu chiefs and African military leaders. Although Senzangakhona then married her, Nandi was condemned as a disgrace by the Zulu and the Langeni, both because of her pregnancy and because she and her husband were considered too closely related to be married. Abuse at the hands of the Zulu forced Nandi and Shaka to return to her tribe, only to be cast out once more during the famine of 1802. They then found refuge with the Mthethwa people, whose chief Dingiswayo was in the process of creating a powerful military state. Shaka proved to be a fearless warrior and rose through the ranks of the Mthethwa army, being named by Dingiswayo as his successor before Dingiswayo's assassination in 1817. Senzangakhona died around 1815, and Shaka soon claimed the chieftainship of the Zulu by mere force. Nandi's close relationship with her son, who never married, gave her unheard-of power. Reputed to have been bad-tempered even before her misfortunes, she was called Ndlorukazi, "The Great She Elephant," and used her position to take revenge on her enemies. Under Shaka's rule, the Zulu became extremely powerful, even legendary, military force, some 40,000 strong; his establishment of all-female regiments has been attributed to the example set for him by his warrior-mother.

Nandi died in 1827. Shaka ordered a time of public mourning during which no crops could be planted, all milk was to be poured out, and all pregnant women killed. He ordered his mother's young handmaidens to be placed with her in the grave, and he set 12,000 soldiers to guard it for a year. Summary executions set off a massacre that claimed the lives of some 7,000 people in the course of three month. The terror stopped when **Mekabayi**, a close friend and sister-in-law of Nandi's, plotted a successful coup carried out by Shaka's half-brother Dingane who assassinated Shaka and took over the chieftainship in 1828.

Summary

It's no big secret that Africa is home to many great safaris, wildlife conservation and ancient wonders the world has ever known, but if you ever plan on traveling there for these kinds of vacations in the near future, you might want to consider what African cities have to offer. There are lavish 5-star hotels to boot and restaurants featuring the best in African cuisine, shopping malls, cultural centers, live entertainment, sports, amphitheater, public parks, zoos and top rated Universities and the most beautiful botanical gardens. I could go on but I'm inclined to stick close to the topic matter of this book.

However, may I impose this question: Wouldn't it be nice if people started visiting Africa for what its urban cities have to offer? There are many beautiful cities that are great vacation destinations inside Africa that hold great cultural centers, zoo's, monuments, artifacts, and many trade opportunities and are fun and safe to visit. And may I ask one final question: Did you know that there are increasing numbers of middle class living in African cities? Jobs and business opportunities are wide open in African cities and now more than ever you can connect with its people via the internet. So don't turn your back on Africa, discover all the beauty it has to offer. Rather than buying tickets to go only on a safari trip, start exploring what African cities has to offer in its urban modernization.

Annotated

1. Wikipedia content contributor – Each African Cities

2. Wikipedia content contributor – Ref. Kings & Queen of Africa

3. Wikipedia Free Encyclopedia -

The content for African cities relied heavily on references provided by public domain in particular: en.wikipadia.org. We encourage our reader to follow up with further research of their own through the reliable online sources above. While the information in this book can be found through public domain sources, African cities is the focus of 22 developed cities on the continent of Africa that uniquely contrast Westerner's (U.S) views when they come to think of Africa, I also attempted to explore ancient civilization through the same lens to help our readers look beyond the volume of miss-representation of Africa that has been push so widely in the past and present media.

Look for our upcoming new book, Coming Soon:

Kings & Queens of Africa: From Ancient to modern day Civilization.

African City Poster Map

(Classroom Educational supplement)

Available: Great for Schools/Institutions

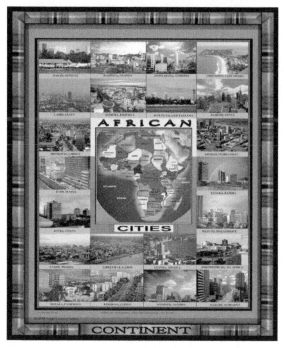

24x36

Colorful as it is Beautiful.

Eye Catching, Pictures of urban cities on the continent of

Africa

AfricanCitytravel.com/prints

Coming Soon:

To learn more about urban cities on the Continent of Africa go to: AfricanCitiesWorldStudy.com

Find information on; Cities – Culture – Cuisine – Travel – Art and more.

RECOMMENDATION:

Traveling & Vacation Plans –.AfricanCityTravel.com

Recommended: reading/topics and sites, see:

FriendsoftheAfricanUnion.com

Akon: Lighting up Africa initiated

Nick Cannon: Films about Black Kings& Queens of Africa.

Africa.com (News and trends in modern day Africa)

AfricanDiasporadirectorate.org

African Cities with the greatest Safari get away

South Africa Safari and cities tours

Africa fastest growing cities

15 best cities to live in Africa

Opray Winfrey *Leadership Academy for Girls*

African Wildlife Foundation (awf.org)

Great Kings and Queens of Africa

BlackTriumph.com (Focus on Black Accomplishment)

AfricanCityWorldStudy.com / AfricanCityTravel.com

To re-order book go to: Amazon.com

African Cities "What Comes To Mind When You think of Africa"

By: Napolean Givens

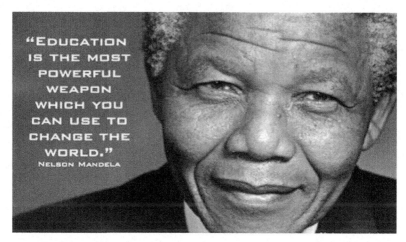

"EDUCATION IS THE MOST POWERFUL WEAPON WHICH YOU CAN USE TO CHANGE THE WORLD."
NELSON MANDELA

Sources: The contents of this book has been gathered through reliable sources: Wikipedia and other reliable African government sources.

African cities can serve as a great reference and classroom textbook for beginners. Begin classroom discussion asking students: What comes to mind when they think of Africa. Use the African Cities Poster to excite interest and discussion. Have your students pick a city to do an essay as part of their classroom assignment using this textbook and other free study resources. The African Cities Poster Map will help to stimulate student's interest in learning. Have students to contrast how they think Africa is being portrayed in America media or miss represented. Ask what their research tells them in light of what they may have read or learn about Africa?

Though Africa has its problems, as does every nation on planet earth, it's an abundantly rich continent that's full of natural minerals world's nations depend on to function. And although its continent been exploited for decades, Africa has turned the corner in urban cities modernization and economy the likes that have never been seen before. Africa is the *new land* of opportunity that is wide open for anyone to gain economically. Now is the time to make Africa your friend and a place to go discover all it has to offer in modern day cities. From the cradle of our ancient civilization to urban cities modernization, Africa awaits each of us to help it fulfill the world needs.

Made in the USA
Middletown, DE
10 February 2021